# NORMAN GILLER

# THE GOLDEN MILERS

**NORMAN GILLER**

# THE GOLDEN MILERS

CHARTWELL
BOOKS, INC.

First published in United States by
Chartwell Books, a division of
Book Sales Inc.,
110 Enterprise Avenue,
Seacaucas,
New Jersey, 07094,
U.S.A.

ISBN 0 89009 531 0

Produced by Winchmore Publishing
Services Ltd.,
48 Lancaster Avenue,
Hadley Wood,
Herts, England.

Designed by Roy Williams
Edited by Sue Butterworth

Printed in Hong Kong by Lee Fung Asco
Ltd.

# CONTENTS

# FOREWORD

THE SPECTACULAR SUCCESSES of Coe and Ovett, or should I say Ovett and Coe, have rekindled public enthusiasm for athletics. They have written a new but not final chapter in the history of the mile race. Norman Giller has given their feats historical perspective and, using his expert knowledge and the interest which first attracted him to sports writing, has added flesh and spirit to the bare bones of these records. I hope his book will inspire the next generation of British athletes to outstrip their latest world record heroes.

It is interesting to speculate why the intrinsically simple and unimportant act of placing one foot after another for 1,760 yards as fast as possible should have become an almost pre-eminent sporting achievement. I believe the appeal lies in its very simplicity. It needs no money, no equipment, no particular physique, no knowledge and no education. But in a world of increasingly complex technology it appears to stand out as a naïve statement about the nature of man. With his own two feet a man can set out and overcome difficulties inside and outside himself to reach a pinnacle upon which he can declare, 'No one ever did that before'. The thought is almost banal; the word 'challenge' is over used but, especially to the young, such acts have a profound reality.

The startling progress in the mile record in recent years has in part been the result of synthetic tracks and better designed running shoes, but has come about mainly because of much harder training. It also makes medical sense for young athletes to expose (but not over-expose) themselves to the stresses of running in adolescence before physiques are fully formed.

The last chapter of the story of the mile race cannot yet be written. A young reader may well find inspiration as well as instruction in these pages. I was fired by seeing Sydney Wooderson, and others will be enthralled by the whole history of the mile race, so well described here. After reading it, you may stop and ponder on the possibility of a 3½-minute mile!

Sir Roger Bannister

*Jules Ladoumegue . . . the first man to break the 4 min 10 sec mile barrier. The 'Flying Frenchman' also had the distinction of becoming the first man to break the 3 min 50 sec barrier in the 1,500 metres.*

# THE FORERUNNERS

## 4 01.4

# THE FORERUNNERS

THE MILE IS DERIVED from an ancient Roman measure of 1,000 paces and has become a long Roman road down which the greatest middle-distance runners in athletics history have been drawn like hungry men to a feast. Even in this metric age, no other race quite captures the attention and imagination of spectators and athletes alike as does the mile. The *Golden* mile. Since the four-minute barrier was first splintered and then smashed by the great modern milers, it has continued to lure the world's finest runners bidding to produce the ultimate, *unbeatable* mile performance.

For the last hundred years, each generation has discovered at least one master miler who has set new standards for his successors. In that time, the world record has come tumbling down from Walter George's 4 min 19.4 sec in 1882 to Sebastian Coe's scorching 3 min 47.33 sec in 1981. The same improvement over the next hundred years would

mean the super-human record holder in 2082 running the mile in a mind-blowing 3 min 15.26 sec. That would call for four laps each covered at an average of 48.81 seconds. There were ten record-breaking forerunners who led the way to Roger Bannister's historic, first four-minute mile in 1954; the first of them was *Walter George* (4 min 19.4 sec), the 'Wiltshire Wonder', who made a series of carefully planned assaults on the magnetic mile. He followed quickly in the footsteps of fellow-Briton Walter Slade who had set the world's best at 4 min 24.5 sec in 1875.

George was out on his own, devising training methods that gave him physical-fitness superiority over all his contemporaries. He broke world records from one mile to 10 miles and also set a world's best by covering 11 miles 932 yards in an hour on 28 July 1884. Born in Calne, Wiltshire in 1858 (he died and was buried there in 1943), George first lowered the world mark to 4 min 23.2

sec on 16 August 1880. He then broke the 4 min 20 sec barrier with a run of 4 min 19.4 sec on 3 June 1882, and knocked a second off this time two years later.

Also famous for his speed on a penny-farthing bicycle, George turned professional in 1885 to challenge Scotsman William Cummings who was the one man in the world anywhere near his class. They met in a special mile race on 23 August 1886. The venue was Lillie Bridge, which was the setting for the second FA Cup Final in 1873 and west London's major stadium before the building nearby of Stamford Bridge. George ran four even-paced laps to win in a remarkable 4 min 12.75 sec, an unofficial world record that no amateur or professional could improve on for a period of 29 years.

*John Paul Jones,* a student at Cornell University, set the first world record ratified by the newly-formed International Amateur Athletics Association on 31 May 1913. He clocked 4 min 14.4

*Frenchman Henri de Fleurac shows the loping style that was popular with milers in the first quarter of the century. He carries hand weights as a training aid.*

*American Abel Kiviat leads Frenchman Arnaud in the 1,500 metres final at the 1912 Olympics in Stockholm. The race was won by Britain's Arnold Jackson who is poised for his victory sprint in third place.*

sec when winning the Intercollegiate championship for a third successive year. This lowered the previous best time by Irish American Thomas Conneff who in 1895 had recaptured the world record from Britain's Fred Bacon with a time of 4 min 15.6 sec.

Another American student, *Norman Taber,* had given notice of his potential when he took the bronze medal in the 1912 1,500 metres final behind Britain's Arnold Jackson and U.S. team-mate Abel Kiviat. John Paul Jones finished fourth in a blanket finish to the final and he and Taber became America's outstanding milers in the years immediately before America's entry into the First World War. Running in a specially framed handicap race on 16 July 1915, Taber reduced the world record to 4 min 12.6 sec. His performance was achieved on the same Cambridge, Massachusetts, track where his great rival John Paul Jones had set his record two years earlier.

# THE FORERUNNERS

Paavo Nurmi's remarkable long-running career spanned more than 20 years and included 22 world record performances. Here he trails fellow Finn Lauri Virtanen during a 10,000 metres race in Turku in 1932 that he won with a devastating sprint finish.

*Paavo Nurmi, the legendary 'Phantom Finn', leads Frenchman Joseph Guillemot in the 5,000 metres final at the 1920 Olympics in Antwerp. Guillemot stunned the Finn by handing him a rare defeat. Nurmi gained revenge by beating Guillemot in the 10,000 metres.*

Eight years later the legendary 'Phantom Finn', *Paavo Nurmi,* shattered the world record with a 4 min 10.4 sec run in Stockholm on 23 August 1923. Born in Turku in 1897, Paavo Johannes Nurmi revolutionised middle-distance running and set new standards and peaks not only for performances on the track but also for training. He was like a time machine, running with a stopwatch in his hand, as he paced himself to a long procession of world records. During a long-running career that spanned more than 20 years, he set 22 world records for distances between 1,500 metres and 20 kilometres, and won six individual Olympic gold medals and three team-event gold medals, a story of supremacy unrivalled on the track.

It was Nurmi who launched an army of milers on an assault on the 4 min 10 sec mile barrier, and a Frenchman, *Jules Ladoumegue,* finally broke that barrier. Ladoumegue came to world prominence when he collected a silver medal in the 1,500 metres final at the 1928 Amsterdam Olympics. It was the prelude to a remarkable double. On 5

October 1930, he had the distinction of becoming the first man to break the 3 min 50 sec barrier in the 1,500 metres with a time of 3 min 49.2 sec. Running in Paris virtually a year later in a specially staged mile race, he became the first man to duck under 4 min 10 sec with an impressive 4 min 9.2 sec.

Few people realised the potential of *John (Jack) Lovelock* when he finished seventh in the 1932 Los Angeles Olympics. It was after switching from Otago University to Oxford for his pre-medical degree that he laid the foundation for a great tradition of New Zealand middle-distance runners (see *Peter Snell* and *John Walker*). Representing a combined Oxford and Cambridge team at Prince-

*Jules Ladoumegue . . . on his way to a remarkable world record-breaking double triumph.*

*Jack Lovelock ... breaking the tape and the world record in the 1936 Olympic 1,500 metres final and (left) relaxing before competing for Oxford against Cambridge at Fenners in 1932.*

ton on 15 July 1933, he beat highly-rated United States star Bill Bonthron by six yards for a new mile world record of 4 min 7.6 sec. Lovelock then quietly went back to concentrating on his studies, moving to London Hospital and keeping a low athletics profile as he prepared without fuss for the 1936 Berlin Olympics. Wearing the distinctive all-black strip of New Zealand, he was content to take a back-marker place in the 1,500 metres final as the high-quality field sped through the first lap on a world record pace. His tactics were planned to perfection and he confounded all his rivals with a devastating sprint 300 metres out and powered away to win in a world record 3 min 47.8 sec.

It was the final big race for Lovelock who retired from major athletics to concentrate on his medical work. He qualified as a doctor at St Mary's Hospital, London, which was where some 20 years later Sir Roger Bannister – the world's first four-minute miler – also studied medicine. In 1940 Lovelock fell off a horse while out riding and sustained serious head injuries that affected his eyesight. He died tragically in New York on 29 December 1949, when he fell under a subway car at Church Avenue Station. He was six days off his fortieth birthday.

The next of the classic milers was *Glenn Cunningham* whose bold front-running style earned him the nickname 'The Iron Horse of Kansas'. Along with countrymen Bill Bonthron, Gene Venzke and Archie San Romani, Canadian Phil Edwards, New Zealander Jack Lovelock, Italian Luigi Beccali and Britain's Sydney Wooderson, he helped turn the mile into the glamour event of the 1930s when a series of 'miles of the century'

*Luigi Beccali ... the Italian ace who helped turn the mile into the glamour event of the 1930s. He was the 1932 Olympic 1,500 metres gold medallist.*

attracted world-wide attention. In seven years of racing at top level, Cunningham ran more than 20 sub-4 min 10 sec mile races. He finished fourth in the 1,500 metres in the 1932 Olympics, and took the silver medal behind Lovelock in the 1936 Berlin Games when they both finished inside Bill Bonthron's world record. He produced his peak performance on 16 June 1934, when he outsprinted his great rival Bonthron to lower Jack Lovelock's

*Left: Sydney Wooderson...one of Britain's most popular sporting heroes.*

*Right: Arne Andersson leads Gundar 'The Wonder' Haegg (No. 1) in one of their wartime duels in Sweden in 1942. Haegg won this two mile race in 8 min 47.8 sec – one of 10 world records he set in a span of just 82 days.*

world mile record to 4 min 6.8 sec on the same Princeton track where the New Zealander had triumphed 11 months earlier. His fastest mile run came indoors, where he was a master on the tight bends. He clocked 4 min 4.4 sec in the winter of 1934. Cunningham was known as a 'miracle man' of the track. At the age of seven, he was badly burned in a school fire that killed his brother. Surgeons considered amputating his legs, but after treatment, which lasted for twelve months, he was able to leave hospital. He took up running for therapeutic exercise.

Off and on the track, *Sydney Wooderson* looked the least likely man to be a world beater. He stood just 5 ft 6 in, weighed less than nine-stone and wore thick-rimmed glasses. In an era when the blond Lovelock and the muscular Cunningham were at their peak, he managed to match – and sometimes master – them with gritty performances that made him one of Britain's most popular sporting heroes. A leg injury that required an operation prevented him from showing his best form in the 1936 Olympics, but a world record 4 min 6.4 sec mile in a specially framed handicap race at Motspur Park, Surrey, on 8 August 1937, proved his enormous ability. The following year he set world records at 800 metres and 880 yards and won the European 1,500 metres championship in Paris. Eight years later, at the age of 31, he won the European 5,000 metres title in Oslo before retiring to concentrate on his career as a solicitor. The little man was a giant in the eyes of the public and his middle-distance rivals for more than a decade.

The Second World War put an end to the world record ambitions of many athletes, but in neutral Sweden the race went on and *Gundar Haegg* and his compatriot *Arne Andersson* kept up a non-stop barrage on the four-minute mile barrier. Each broke or equalled the world record three times as they pushed each other to new frontiers but, try as they might, never under the magical four minutes. It was like running into an invisible wall. Andersson got his best time down to 4 min 1.6 sec in Malmo on 18 July 1944. A year and a day later, Haegg reduced the record to 4 min 1.4 sec on the same Malmo track. An astonishing sequence of victories in 1942 earned Haegg the nickname 'Gundar the Wonder'. In a span of 82 days between 1 July and 20 September, he won 32 successive races and broke ten world records ranging from 1,500 metres (3 min 45.8 sec) to 5,000 metres (13 min 58.2 sec).

Incredibly, neither Haegg nor Andersson won a major championship. Both were setting their sights on the 1946 European championships and 1948 Olympics when they were banned for infringements of the amateur code. They were forced into retirement with the four-minute mile still beyond them. 'It is going to take somebody very special to beat the barrier,' said Gundar. 'But it *will* be beaten, of that I am quite sure.' All it would need was the right time, the right place, the right pace and, most important of all, that 'very special' athlete . . .

*Roger Bannister . . . the first man to break the four-minute barrier.*

# ROGER
# BANNISTER
## 3 59.4

THE FOUR-MINUTE MILE barrier was considered the 'unconquerable Everest' of athletics when 25-year-old medical student Roger Bannister was called to his marks at the Iffley Road track, Oxford, on the wet and windy evening of Thursday, 6 May 1954. Just 3 minutes 59.4 seconds later he hurled himself almost despairingly through the tape and into sporting legend.

In these days of sub-3 min 50 sec miles, it might be difficult to fathom what all the fuss was about. But what needs to be stressed is that until this historic run by Bannister, the four-minute mile had become as much a psychological barrier as a physical one. For years, the world's greatest middle-distance runners had been punishing themselves in their attempts to duck under four minutes but they were continually beaten by the clock. It took Bannister to unlock the door through which a long procession of milers have since followed. Yet the race in which he was to make world-wide headlines was very nearly abandoned as a record attempt. Bannister had prepared and planned for the race throughout the winter, driven on by the knowledge that Australian John Landy and American Wes Santee were both plotting barrier-breaking runs. Beating four minutes was one target but being the *first* to do it was even more important. Who remembers the man who was second to conquer Mount Everest after Edmund Hillary?

Advised by Austrian-born coach Franz Stampfl, Bannister trained for the most important race of his life with Achilles Club colleagues Chris Brasher and Chris Chataway. He conditioned his mind as well as his body, adopting a single-minded attitude that had triggered criticism in the past from people who did not share his vision and accused him of being too much of a lone wolf. He proved to be an antelope in wolf's clothing. Bannister, a sensitive, withdrawn personality who was happiest away from the crowds rock-climbing or on country walks, had made a silent promise to himself three years earlier to one day try to break the four-minute barrier on the Iffley Road track that could have been called 'The Track that Bannister Built.' It was while President of the Oxford University Athletic Club that he fought and won a battle to get the old ⅓-mile track replaced with a new six-lane 440 yards circuit conforming to international specifications.

He selected the annual AAA v Oxford University match as the stage for his record attempt. May was not the ideal month and the cramped Iffley Road stadium hardly seemed the right setting for such an historic race. But he knew he had to grab this opportunity before Landy and Santee launched their record bids in other parts of the world where the weather and track conditions were more conducive to sustained fast running. The AAA v Oxford match usually had about as much impact on the general public as a village fete, but rumours of the record assault leaked out and a stadium that was usually deserted filled with spectators eager to see athletics history in the making. An indication of the bad conditions that awaited Bannister, Brasher and Chataway, is that when they arrived at the track the spectators were dressed in raincoats and sheltered under umbrellas as wind and rain lashed the tiny stadium. They were on the point of abandoning the record bid when the rain stopped and the wind dropped. Operation Four Minutes was back on.

Bannister, his 6 ft 1 in, 10 st 11 lb frame prepared to a peak, had only one real opponent: the clock. Everybody else in the six-man field was as keen as he himself was to see the barrier broken. As the starter called them to their marks, he took several deep breaths to try to control his jangling nerves. The runners were so affected by tension that there was a false start but they got away at the second time of asking and, as pre-arranged, the bespectacled Brasher raced to the front as pacemaker. Bannister, wound up like a giant spring, thought the pace was too slow and shouted 'faster!' to Brasher who kept his head and the correct speed. He took them through the first quarter in 57.4 sec and hit the half-mile mark in a bang-on-schedule 1 min 58 sec.

Chataway, red-haired and barrel-chested, overtook Brasher halfway round lap three and gamely made his contribution to the record by maintaining the pace in the tough no man's land area where so many four-minute mile bids had floundered in the past. Bannister, with his seemingly effortless long stride, was eating up the ground at Chataway's heels, looking relaxed and totally in command of the situation. Had any of the 1,200 crowd been able to take their eyes off the fascinating race they would have seen a lingering double rainbow decorating the slate-grey sky and the clock on the nearby church steeple showing nine minutes after six.

*Roger Bannister, who unlocked the door through which a procession of milers have since followed.*

*Opposite: The young Bannister winning the AAA half-mile title at London's White City in 1952 (left) and competing for Oxford against London University in a mile race at Motspur Park in 1949 when he was beaten by 1948 Olympic finalist John Parlett.*

*The historic moment when the clock stopped at 3 min 59.4 sec.*

But all eyes were on the front two runners on the track and the only clocks on anybody's minds were the stopwatches in the hands of the timekeepers ranged alongside the finishing line.

The bell signalling the last lap and Bannister's date with destiny rang as Chataway completed three-quarters of a mile in 3 min 0.4 sec. Bannister was timed at 3 min 0.5 sec. He had to run the last 440 yards in 59.4 sec to break the 'impossible' barrier. Chataway, drained chalk white by his exertions, started to falter and coming off the next bend with 230 yards to go Bannister unleashed his famous finishing 'kick'. He moved up a gear and swept majestically past Chataway with a stunning surge of speed that made his Achilles clubmate look as if he was suddenly running backwards. The roar of the crowd was like a gale-force wind at Bannister's back as they urged him on in his long, lonely drive for the tape and the permanency of the record book. In the last desperate 100 yards, he was

fighting through a fog of fatigue, a biting cross wind and a fear that his long legs would betray him on the threshold of one of the great moments in athletics history. With a super human effort, he virtually leapt through the tape and fell semi-conscious into the arms of the Reverend Nicholas Stacey who was an Oxford University sprinter and his close friend. He had given all he had got and was now totally exhausted.

Norris McWhirter, distinguished Editor of the *Guinness Book of Records* who probably knows more about records than any other man on earth, was on duty as the results announcer. He added to the agonising suspense in the stadium with the following drawn-out race result: 'Ladies and gentlemen, here is the result of event number nine, the one mile: First, number forty-one, R. G. Bannister, of the Amateur Athletic Association and formerly of Exeter and Merton Colleges, with a time which is a new meeting and track record and

*Coach Franz Stampfl (left) congratulates Bannister after his exhausting run into the unknown.*

which, subject to ratification will be a new English native, British national, British all comers', European, British Empire and World record. The time is THREE . . .'

The roar of the crowd drowned the rest of the announcement. The spectators had heard all that mattered: 'Three . . .'. The exact time was 3 min 59.4 sec. The barrier had been broken. The 'impossible' had been proved possible. Suddenly Roger Bannister's was the most famous name in sport and he was feted and acclaimed around the world. He carried his fame with great dignity and natural modesty and became a fine ambassador for British

sport in general and athletics in particular. Much later, with time to compose his thoughts and feelings, Bannister recorded in his absorbing book *First Four Minutes* (Putnam, 1955): 'It was a triumph not only for me but also for Chris Brasher and Chris Chataway. We shared a place where no man had yet ventured, secure for all time no matter how fast men might run miles in the future. We had done it how we wanted, where we wanted and just when we wanted at our first attempt of the year . . .' Of the final 200 yards of the race, he wrote: 'I had a moment of mixed joy and anguish, when my mind took over. It raced well ahead of my body and

*The three miling musketeers after the first four-minute mile: Chris Brasher (left), Bannister and Chris Chataway.*

Bannister is honoured as Europe's 'Athlete of the Year' at a Variety Club luncheon at London's Savoy Hotel in April 1955. Making the presentation is Harold Abrahams whose own Olympic gold medal performance on the track was featured in the film Chariots of Fire.

The final fling . . . Bannister wins the European 1,500 metres title in the last race of his career at Berne in 1954.

drew my body compellingly forward. I felt that the moment of a lifetime had come. There was no pain, only a great unity of movement and aim. The world seemed to stand still, or did not exist. The only reality was the next two hundred yards of track under my feet. The tape meant finality – extinction perhaps.'

Cynics, armed with the times of today's golden milers, could scoff at what may appear over-dramatic statements. But Bannister *had* been where no man had been before him. He performed his feat more than a quarter of a century ago but his performance continues to stand out above all others, simply because he was the *first*. It was Roger Bannister who showed the way. Everybody else could only follow.

# FOR THE RECORD

Roger Bannister was born at Harrow on 23 March 1929. His father was a civil servant. As an 18-year-old under-graduate at Oxford University, he turned down an invitation to train for a possible place in the British team for the 1948 Olympics. With a single-minded attitude that was to become his hallmark, he set his sights on the 1,500 metres title in the 1952 Helsinki Olympics. These Games were to bring him his biggest disappointment. His calculations were turned upside down when an extra round of heats were included at the last moment. He was not mentally or physically prepared for this and his finishing strength deserted him in the Final when he came in a creditable, but bitterly dejected, fourth.

He was three times AAA mile champion – 1951 (4 min 07.8 sec), 1953 (4 min 05.2 sec) and 1954 (4 min 07.6 sec). In 1952, he won the AAA 880 yards title in 1 min 51.5 sec. He was a member of the Great Britain 4 x 1 mile relay team

which broke the world record with a time of 16 min 41.0 sec in August 1953.

His first mile victory was in the Freshmen's Sports at Oxford in 1946. His time: 4 min 53.0 sec. His fastest mile run was when he clocked 3 min 58.8 sec, winning the British Empire Games mile title in Vancouver in 1954 (see *John Landy* chapter).

He won the European 1,500 metres gold medal in the final race of his career at Berne on 29 August 1954. His time was a championship record: 3 min 43.8 sec.

He became Doctor Roger Bannister in 1954 and now works as a respected consultant neurologist practising in London. Made a CBE in 1955, he continued to give his time to sport as chairman of the Sports Council. In 1975 he was knighted for his services to sport.

*John Landy, the second man to break the four-minute mile barrier.*

# JOHN
# LANDY
### 3 57.9

JOHN LANDY WAS ONE of the greatest but also one of the unluckiest milers of all time. Like his fellow Australian, Ron Clarke, a decade later, he got into the habit of beating the clock but – when it really mattered – not the opposition. Landy had seemed the man most likely to be first to break the four-minute barrier. He unleashed a sequence of spectacular solo runs during the 1953-54 season in Australia, little knowing that his performances were giving an Englishman called Roger Bannister extra motivation to step up his winter training.

After getting to within a fraction of Gunda Haegg's seven-year-old world record for a sixth time in April 1954, Landy announced his intention to bid for a four-minute mile during a Scandinavian tour in June. By the time he reached Europe, he found himself bidding to become the *second* man to break the barrier. Bannister beat him to it by just 46 days. It was the difference for Landy between being just another outstanding miler (along with Wooderson, Lovelock, Andersson and Haegg) and being immortalised. Chris Chataway was a common denominator in the races in which Bannister and then Landy ducked under four minutes for the first time. He helped set the pace for Bannister and was the man who pushed Landy through the barrier in Turku, Finland, on 21 June 1954.

Landy preferred to lead from gun to tape, killing off the opposition with a sustained near-sprint pace. These tactics took him close to the 'magical' four-minute mile in four races in Finland but he lacked the sort of opposition that could give him the final push he needed to break the barrier. Then Chataway volunteered to take him on, confident that he could hang on the Australian's heels and then outsprint him off the final bend with a kick finish that was almost in the Bannister class.

Landy and Chataway circled the Turku track as if roped together, with the future British Government Minister forcing the pace from the back of the tandem. Unaccustomed to having anybody still with him at the bell, Landy pushed the accelerator and found untapped finishing speed. He went through 1,500 metres in a world record 3 min 41.8 sec and sliced through the tape at the end of the mile in an astonishing 3 min 57.9 sec. The dual record run was a triumph for Landy's perseverance and for the punishing training techniques of eccentric Australian coach Percy Cerutty. Now the stage

was set for the 'Mile of the Century' between the two golden milers, Bannister and Landy.

They lined up against each other six weeks later in the British Empire Games' mile final in Vancouver on the afternoon of Saturday 7 August 1954. The bookmakers made Landy a 4-1 favourite, not appreciating how the British doctor had planned and prepared for the confrontation with meticulous care. There was a stark contrast in the personalities, physiques and race preparations of the two rivals. Bannister was tall and pale, painfully shy and a deep thinker who believed running was as much about having the mental attitude right as the physical fitness. His adviser Franz Stampfl concentrated on stoking up his confidence and the competitive aggressiveness that had been lacking in his make-up. Landy was the complete opposite, a stocky, sun-bronzed figure with short, black curly hair and a bouncing, friendly personality. While Bannister seemed to find running hard work, the Australian loved every second on and off the track. The harder his coach Cerutty pushed him the better he liked it and onlookers watching him on runs – often bare footed – at the Vancouver training camp were convinced they were watching the next Empire Games champion. He was happy to work out in the full view of the world's press, while Bannister trained away from the main centre and in secret. The 'experts' interpreted Bannister's reluctance to perform in the public spotlight as a lack of confidence and many of them wrote him off as having no chance of victory. Landy, they figured, would simply run the finish out of the introverted Briton. They failed to understand Bannister's totally single-minded approach to running. Underneath the shy exterior, there was a steely competitor and he had a carefully calculated victory plan worked out.

The race was a classic that more than lived up to expectations. Both Bannister and Landy went into it with secret, nagging worries. Bannister was handicapped by a severe cold and Landy was suffering from a cut foot after stepping on broken glass the night before the final. But they shrugged off their troubles and both provided peak performances. Predictably, Landy took the lead soon after the gun and set a searing pace. He completed the first lap in 58 seconds, with Bannister five yards back in second place. At the halfway mark, reached in 1 min 58.2 sec, few among the 35,000 capacity crowd, sweltering under a scorching sun, would have given Bannister any chance of winning the race. Landy had stretched his lead to a dozen yards and was looking strong and confident. But instead of panicking, Bannister gradually increased his tempo and when Landy entered the last lap at 2 min 58.4 sec the Englishman was striding along just four yards away.

Now their differing styles were accentuated as Landy stepped up the pressure, his shuffling steps becoming quicker and more urgent in contrast to the giant, loping strides of the gangling Bannister. Landy went through the 1,500 metres mark just 0.1 sec outside the world record he had set in Finland. Coming off the final bend, the Australian cast an anxious glance over his left shoulder to try to gauge his lead. It no longer existed. At this precise moment, Bannister launched his attack on the outside and burst to the front in the split second when Landy was looking for him. In those final, glorious for Bannister and heart-breaking for Landy, 80 yards, the Englishman stretched his lead to five yards and collapsed through the tape in what had become characteristic style. He was clocked at 3 min 58.8 sec. Landy followed him across the line in 3 min 59.6 sec, the first time two runners had beaten four minutes in the same race.

Twenty minutes later, the 'Race of the Century' was sadly overshadowed by one of the sporting dramas of the century. Marathon leader Jim Peters came reeling into the stadium like a drunken man,

a pathetic puppet of a figure who could get no co-ordination into his movements. Sixteen runners had started out on the 26 miles and 385 yards route but the boiling-hot conditions had got the better of eight of them and were now about to claim a ninth victim. It took Peters eleven agonising minutes to cover 200 of the remaining 385 yards to the tape. He fell to the track six times, staggered and crawled and scrambled along on a zig-zag course to nowhere. Finally he collapsed across what his be-mused brain convinced him was the finishing line – but it was 185 yards away on the other side of the track. Nobody among the horrified onlookers had dared help him because just a touch would have brought instant disqualification as in Pietro Dorando's infamous Marathon run in the 1908 Olympic Games (he collapsed four times inside the White City Stadium and was helped across the line by two officials). Peters was borne off on a stretcher and was put in an oxygen tent for seven hours and fed intravenously with saline and glucose. The 35-year-old optician from Essex, England's team captain, later regained full fitness – but never raced again.

Bannister and Landy had watched the sickening spectacle from the centrefield where they had just collected their medals. It threw a dark cloud over their momentous duel which even now, approaching 30 years later, stands up to the billing it got at the time as 'The Mile of the Century'.

# FOR THE RECORD

John Landy was born at Hawthorn, Victoria, on 4 April 1930. His first love was football until Australian coach Percy Cerutty spotted his potential and guided him towards an eventful and distinguished athletics career. He first came to international prominence in 1952 when he was runner-up in both the 880 yards and one mile in the Australian championships. His inexperience at top level was exposed in the 1952 Helsinki Olympics when he failed to get through the first heats in the 1,500 metres (beaten by Roger Bannister) and 5,000 metres.

Landy 'came of age' as a miler in December 1952, when he clocked 4 min 2.1 sec on a rough dirt track in Australia. Cerutty's punishing training schedules were beginning to pay dividends. Over the next 14 months he ran six one mile races in times under 4 min 3 sec leading up to his world record 3 min 57.9 sec in Finland in June 1954.

He took a season's breather after the disappointment of being beaten by Bannister in the 1954 Empire Games'

mile final but made a spectacular return to action in 1955, breaking four-minutes for the mile in four races and winning a three-mile race in an impressive 13 min 27.4 sec. Landy's target was the gold medal in the 1,500 metres in the 1956 Melbourne Olympics. He was given the honour of taking the Olympic oath on behalf of the competitors and there would have been no more popular winner in the Games had he been able to win a title.

Landy reached the 1,500 metres final that included four other sub-four minute milers. He switched from his usual front running tactics, lying seventh in a tightly bunched field at the bell. He unleashed one of the fastest finishes of his career but left it too late and was beaten to the tape by Irishman Ronnie Delany and German Klaus Richtzenhain.

For Landy, there was the consolation of a bronze medal and the knowledge that he was admired and respected throughout the world of athletics as one of the greatest milers ever seen.

*Derek Ibbotson . . . the laughing cavalier of the track.*

# DEREK
# IBBOTSON
## 3 57.2

DEREK IBBOTSON TACKLED his athletics like he tackled life – with bubbling exuberance and good humour mixed in with a tough competitive spirit that typified his Yorkshire breeding. Many people, including his rivals, often misinterpreted his happy-go-lucky approach as reflecting a lack of total commitment. But when it really mattered, there was no harder trainer or more determined and dedicated a competitor than the likeable 'Ibbo'.

He had stamina to go with his basic speed and first exploded on the athletics scene as a potential world beater in 1955. Little known outside club and services athletics, he suddenly came to prominence by winning the Inter-Counties three-mile championship in 13 min 34.6 sec – a startling time that knocked half-a-minute off his previous best for the distance. The following season he revealed he had matured into a world-class middle distance runner by beating Chris Chataway in the AAA three-mile championship with a time of 13 min 32.6 sec. He then cleaved more than four seconds off this time when winning the three-miles in the international event against Czechoslovakia. Few athletes, before or since, have been able to match his appetite for action and just two days later he lined up in the famous Emsley Carr mile, a great status event for milers. His previous mile performances gave no indication of his ability over this

distance and most onlookers thought he was there purely for speed training. But Ibbo was there to win. He improved by more than seven seconds on his personal best, breaking the tape in 3 min 59.4 sec to equal Roger Bannister's British record.

Ibbotson was selected to represent Britain in the 5,000 metres in the 1956 Melbourne Olympics and performed gallantly, finishing third in the final behind Russian 'Iron Man' Vladimir Kuts and the great Gordon 'Puff-Puff' Pirie, Britain's talented but controversial 'rebel without a pause'. His golden year was 1957 when he adopted a 'have spikes will travel' approach to his athletics. He raced more than 70 times, usually winning and always giving spectators value for their entrance money. Ibbotson was not the prettiest sight in athletics. He lacked the gazelle-like grace of a Herb Elliott or the physical presence of the towering Bannister. But he had great charisma and the crowd identified with his whole-hearted endeavour. His arms used to pump across his chest but while he was all bustle and aggression above the waist he was carried along on a stride that was smooth and economical.

He saved his greatest efforts in his all-action year of 1957 for the mile. On 15 June he marked the birth of his first child with a European record of 3 min 58.4 sec in Glasgow. The following month he arrived with only minutes to spare before the heats of the AAA mile championship and, lacking his usual concentration and commitment, failed to qualify for the final. Ibbo shrugged off his disappointment, switched to the three miles and won the title in a United Kingdom record of 13 min 20.8 sec. In the last months of service with the Royal Air Force, he felt in unbeatable form over the four lap course and was anxious to attack the world mile record while at his peak. Around this time I was working on the late, lamented London *Evening News* and was assisting athletics correspondent Terry O'Connor in the organisation of a *News*-sponsored international meeting. Terry wanted a 'dream mile' as the main attraction and I drew up a list of runners that included Olympic 1,500 metres champion Ronnie Delany, Czech 1,500 metres world record holder Stanislav Jungwirth, Ibbotson and his fellow Yorkshireman Ken Wood, the bespectacled 1956 AAA mile champion. Terry, now a respected rugby and athletics writer on the *Daily Mail,* studied my list, smiled and ticked off each runner. He had already arranged for invitations to

*Vladimir Kuts . . . the Russian 'Iron Man' who won the 5,000 and 10,000 metres gold medals in the 1956 Melbourne Olympics.*

3 57.2

'Ibbo' clocks 3 min 59.4 sec to equal Bannister's British mile record at London's White City on 6 August 1956.

*Ibbotson, who brightened athletics with his style and his smile.*

be sent to every one of them and just the prospect of the race made the hair on the back of my neck stand on end.

Terry O'Connor's vision of a great race became reality on a memorable evening at London's White City Stadium on 19 July 1957. Mike Blagrove, a top-quality club athlete, was slipped in as the 'hare' and set a cracking pace. Jungwirth and Delany were the joint favourites but Ibbo destroyed them with a magnificently judged last lap of 56.9 sec. He produced a devastating final furlong in which he moved with the explosive speed of a sprinter. As he flashed through the tape ten yards ahead of Olympic champion Delany the watches were stopped at a new world record 3 min 57.2 sec. It was one of the great mile races of the decade and Delany, Jungwirth and fourth man Ken Wood were also home inside the 'magic' four minutes.

'I didn't run with any particular plan in mind,' Ibbo said later as he downed a celebratory pint or two. 'I just knew I had to be in touch with the leaders at the bell and then I was determined to give it all I'd got. It was a case of win or bust when I set off on the dash for the tape. I had no idea how close Delany and Jungwirth were but with runners of their calibre in the field I knew I daren't relax. It was the sweetest moment of my life when I hit the tape. I realised from the reaction of everybody around me that I'd got the record. I don't know how long it will last because records are there to be beaten. But I'll tell you this, whoever beats it will feel ruddy tired!' The sporting Delany said: 'I have never seen such a devastating finish as Derek produced over the final 220 yards. He went off like a rocket and I had no answer to it. I guessed he had got the record because my heavy legs were telling me that it just had to be one of the fastest miles ever run. It was a magnificent performance and I was proud to have taken part in such a memorable race.'

Few British athletes have ever endeared themselves so much to the British public as Ibbo but he was never again able to recapture the stunning form he showed in this record-shattering performance. He just did not seem to know how to turn down invitations to compete and almost literally ran himself into the ground before the end of the year. In 1958 he became the first man ever to run a mile in exactly four minutes but it was one of his rare triumphs in a year that was one long anti-climax after his spectacular successes of 1957. 'Within a year of my world record run,' he later commented, 'I was yesterday's hero. The headlines no longer praised but criticized.'

Ibbotson began to have weight problems and the high hopes of his supporters that he would succeed Roger Bannister as Empire Games champion at Cardiff in 1958 were wrecked. The gold medal went to a young Australian called Herb Elliott who was also destined to wipe out Ibbotson's world mile record. But Ibbo loved running too much to leave the world stage and in 1962 he produced flashes of his old magic when he switched to the indoor circuit. He set European records on the boards for the two mile and three mile events. When the AAA indoor championships were revived in 1962 after a 23 year gap, Ibbotson's was one of the first names on the roll of honour when he took the two-mile title in 8 min 52.2 sec. Three years later he knocked nearly ten seconds off that time when regaining the championship in 8 min 42.6 sec.

He continued running competitively into the late sixties and in 1966 led Longwood Harriers to a 4 x 1 mile relay British club record. Then he switched to squash and quickly established himself as a County-class player. A light went out on British athletics when Ibbo finally hung up his spikes. He had brightened the scene with his style and his smile. Derek Ibbotson, Golden Miler, was a one-off.

# FOR THE RECORD

Derek Ibbotson was born in Huddersfield on 17 June 1932. He started running in club athletics in 1947 and first made an international impact while competing for the RAF team, winning the 1956 AAA three-miles title in 13 min 32.6 sec. A year later he retained the title, this time wearing a South London Harriers vest and clocking a United Kingdom record 13 min 20.8 sec.

On the way to his world record 3 min 57.2 sec in the mile he also set a personal best of 3 min 41.9 sec for the 1,500 metres. He had wide-ranging ability, with a best mark for 880 yards of 1 min 52.2 sec and a creditable clocking of 28 min 52.0 sec for six miles.

His fastest run over 5,000 metres came in the 1956 Melbourne Olympic final. He took the bronze medal with a time of 13 min 54.4 sec. Russian Vladimir Kuts won in an Olympic record 13 min 39.6 sec, with Britain's Gordon Pirie second in 13 min 50.6 sec.

Ibbotson linked up with Mike Blagrove, P. R. Clark and Brian Hewson for a world record of 16 min 30.6 sec in the 4 x 1 mile relay in London on 27 September 1958.

As well as being the first man to run one mile in exactly four minutes, he was also clocked at exactly eight minutes when setting a personal best over 3,000 metres.

When his distinguished international career was over, Ibbotson returned to club athletics with Longwood Harriers. He was an inspiration to them and, at the age of 34, helped them set a British club record in the 4 x 1 mile relay.

His memorable run of 3 min 57.2 sec for the mile lasted just over a year as a world record but survived in the record books as a United Kingdom best until fellow Yorkshireman Alan Simpson clocked 3 min 56.6 sec on 7 June 1965.

*Herb Elliott . . . the undefeated master miler.*

HERB
# ELLIOTT
3 54.5

# ELLIOTT

EVERY SPORT HAS ITS MASTER, the 'Great Untouchable' respected and revered by his opponents as well as the general public – Jack Hobbs in cricket, Arnold Palmer in golf, Muhammad Ali in boxing and Stanley Matthews in football. In miling, Herb Elliott was The Master. From the age of 16 when he first started taking a serious interest in running until his retirement at the age of 22, Elliott never once lost a mile or 1,500 metres race. He ran 17 sub-four minute miles and became the first man to break the 3 min 55 sec barrier, which was the next natural target after Roger Bannister had destroyed the myth that a four-minute mile was impossible.

Elliott lifted miling almost to an art form. He used to glide around the track, moving with animal-like grace and rhythm that was never out of control even when he was going flat out for the tape. Like his fellow-Australian John Landy, he was a disciple of the eccentric but effective coach Percy Cerutty who added his exclusive brand of physical and mental conditioning to Elliott's startling natural ability. He not only raced the Cerutty way but also *lived* the Cerutty way. 'I am not so much interested in athletics as in achievement,' he told 16-year-old Elliott when the wide-eyed schoolboy first visited his training camp at Portsea on the Mornington Peninsula in Victoria. Few athletes had the stomach for Cerutty's savagely tough training methods which demanded so much of them that they were driven beyond the edge of exhaustion in almost every session under his supervision. He used to insist on his athletes sprinting up giant sandhills to build strength in their legs. They had to lift heavy weights and run marathon distances in long and lonely training work-outs and were told what to eat and when to eat it. The racing was the easy part.

To know Herb Elliott, you first have to know Percy Cerutty. Born in 1895, he was an Australian civil servant who in 1939 was – in his own words – 'at death's door'. He was given a six months leave of absence to help him try to restore his failing health. Driven on by an iron willpower, he began to search for fitness by running on the sand dunes and enjoyed it so much that he decided to start a career in athletics at the age of 45. He became one of Australia's outstanding long-distance runners, setting records at distances of up to 60 miles. At the age of 51 he covered 101 miles in under 24 hours. Once back to full health, he was convinced he had

*Herb Elliott . . . the Master who lifted miling almost to an art form.*

38

discovered conditioning methods that could help top athletes conquer the world and he gave up his job in the civil service to open his training camp at Portsea. Among the first of his protégés was John Landy but it was Herb Elliott who became his most successful and dedicated pupil. White haired and wiry, Cerutty ate only natural, uncooked foods and expected his athletes to do likewise. Many people dismissed him as a crank but the world-beating performances of Elliott proved beyond argument that there was definite method in his apparent madness. Cerutty saw Elliott win a junior mile in 1955 in a time of 4 min 22 sec and stated: 'This boy can be coached to knock half a minute off that time'. Elliott took him up on the claim. It was the start of an incredible partnership.

A year later, at the age of 18, he clocked a junior world mile record of 4 min 4.3 sec. At 19, he ran three sub-four minute miles within 21 days and already had the world record in his sights. He got himself into shape for the 1958 Empire Games in Cardiff with a sequence of three four-minute miles in California, including taking the American championship in 3 min 57.9 sec. Elliott won the half-mile and mile gold medals in the Cardiff Games and then, as a prelude to the fastest mile of his life, won the 880 yards in the British Games in a Commonwealth record 1 min 47.3 sec. Two days later he lined up in Dublin against 1956 Olympic 1,500 metres champion Ronnie Delany, fellow Australians Mervyn Lincoln and Albert Thomas and New Zealand ace Murray Halberg. Thomas led at the end of the first lap in 58.0 sec and hit the half-mile mark in 1 min 58 sec. Then Lincoln took the field through the bell at 2 min 59 sec before Elliott started his surge for home. He left his talented rivals looking on like helpless spectators as he raced away to win by 12 yards in 3 min 54.5 sec, chopping an astonishing 2.7 seconds of Derek Ibbotson's 13-month-old world record. 'The only way to beat him is to tie his legs together,' said a rueful Ronnie Delany. The next evening, Elliott

*Murray Halberg . . . the 1960 Olympic 5,000 metres champion who tackled Herb Elliott in a Dublin mile race to remember.*

returned the compliment to Albert Thomas when, on the same Dublin track, he paced him to a new world record for two miles.

Most athletes would have been content to rest for the remainder of the season – not Elliott. In a quite unbelievable running blitz over a period of 12 days in August and September 1958, he won three 1,500 metres races and two sub-four minute miles. It included a world record 3 min 36 sec 1,500 metres, with previous record holder Stanislav Jungwirth trailing 15 metres behind in second place. By his demanding standards, the next 18 months were uneventful and people were wondering if he had burnt himself out. But Elliott, following the advice of the canny Cerutty, was deliberately keeping a low profile. His long-range target was the 1960 Olympic 1,500 metres gold medal.

In the Rome Games, Elliott produced a performance that many good judges rate the finest ever witnessed in an Olympic track final. On the signal of a flapping white towel held aloft in the crowd by the wizened figure of Percy Cerutty, Elliott majestically strode into the lead in the final with 600 metres to go. Suddenly it was no longer a race but a procession. All the strength and stamina built over the years in hundreds of killing runs up the sand dunes at Portsea paid dividends as Elliott powered to a devastating victory by an almost unbelievable distance of 20 metres over silver medallist Michel Jazy of France. The magnificence of Elliott's run was underlined when his time was announced as a new world and Olympic record of 3 min 35.6 sec.

*Britain's Gordon Pirie (left) ponders on what tactics to use against the relaxed Elliott, who never once lost a mile race. Pirie specialised over longer distances but included a four-minute mile in his gallery of outstanding performances.*

*Elliott is about to power away from Britain's Mike Rawson to win the 1958 AAA half-mile title at London's White City.*

Professional promoters tried to cash in on his tremendous crowd-pulling power by offering him a staggering £90,000 to run in a world-wide series of races but he preferred to bow out with dignity from a sport he graced with his presence. He wound down his career with four more sub-four minute miles in the month immediately after the Olympics and announced his retirement after cantering to victory in a mile in London in May 1961. He was just 22 and still a year or two short of what would have been the peak years for most milers.

I had a memorable conversation in the summer of 1981 with Fleet Street's Peter Wilson. We were together at the Wembley ringside to see Jim Watt's world lightweight championship boxing defence against Alexis Arguello. Peter had seen every miler that mattered over the previous 40 years and I took the opportunity to ask him where Elliott stood in his personal ratings. 'My dear boy, he was simply the greatest of them all. I first saw him run when he was a sixteen-year-old schoolboy in a race in Sydney and I thought then that he was the most exciting prospect I had seen at that age. He more than lived up to my expectations. He had a quality you find in only the great champions. It's called invincibility.'

Peter Wilson, invincible among sportswriters, sadly died before the year was out. I was glad that I had got his assessment of Herb Elliott – a Master judging a Master.

*Elliott acknowledges the applause of the spectators in Rome after his stunning Olympic triumph in the 1,500 metres final.*

# FOR THE RECORD

Herb Elliott was born at Subiaco, Western Australia, on 25 February 1938. This is the remarkable record of his winning performances in major mile and 1,500 metres races.

| DATE | VENUE | TIME (*1,500 metres) |
|---|---|---|
| 12.1.57 | Melbourne | 4 min 6.0 sec (World junior best) |
| 20.2.57 | Melbourne | 4 min 4.3 sec (World junior best) |
| 9.3.57 | Melbourne | 4 min 0.4 sec (Aust championship) |
| 25.1.58 | Melbourne | 3 min 59.9 sec |
| 30.1.58 | Melbourne | 3 min 58.7 sec |
| 15.2.58 | Perth | 3 min 59.6 sec |
| 2.3.58 | Melbourne | 3 min 51.8 sec* |
| 15.3.58 | Brisbane | 4 min 8.8 sec (Aust championship) |
| 16.5.58 | Los Angeles | 3 min 57.8 sec |
| 31.5.58 | Modesto | 4 min 2.7 sec |
| 6.6.58 | Compton | 3 min 58.1 sec |
| 21.6.58 | Bakersfield | 3 min 57.9 sec (USA championship) |
| 26.7.58 | Cardiff | 3 min 59.0 sec (Empire Games) |
| 6.8.58 | Dublin | 3 min 54.5 sec (World record) |
| 28.8.58 | Gothenburg | 3 min 36.0 sec* (World record) |
| 29.8.58 | Malmo | 3 min 58.0 sec |
| 3.9.58 | London | 3 min 55.4 sec |
| 5.9.58 | Oslo | 3 min 37.4 sec.* |
| 14.3.59 | Brisbane | 3 min 58.9 sec |
| 6.2.60 | Bendigo | 3 min 59.8 sec |
| 20.2.60 | Melbourne | 4 min 0.0 sec |
| 5.3.60 | Perth | 4 min 2.1 sec (Aust championship) |
| 4.6.60 | Compton | 3 min 59.2 sec |
| 6.9.60 | Rome | 3 min 35.6 sec (World record) |
| 14.9.60 | London | 3 min 58.6 sec |
| 18.9.60 | Gothenburg | 3 min 38.4 sec* |
| 20.9.60 | Malmo | 3 min 58.6 sec |
| 23.9.60 | Dublin | 3 min 57.0 sec |
| 26.9.60 | London | 3 min 59.8 sec |
| 13.5.61 | London | 4 min 7.2 sec (final mile race) |

In all, Elliott ran in 36 mile races between January 1957 and May 1961. He won every one of them. He also won the nine 1,500 metres races in which he competed. He ran a leg of 4 min 4.6 sec for the Australian squad that broke the world 4 x 1 mile relay world record on 22 March 1959.

*Peter Snell, the 'Man in Black', beats Jamaican George Kerr in the half-mile for the first leg of a double gold medal triumph in the 1962 Commonwealth Games in Perth.*

# PETER
# SNELL
3 54.1

**P**ETER SNELL WAS AN unknown force when he arrived in Rome for the 1960 Olympics as a competitor in the 800 metres. His best time for the distance was a modest 1 min 49.2 sec and it seemed the most he could hope for was a place in the final. But the 'Man in Black' astonished everybody apart from himself and his coach, Arthur Lydiard, by beating world record holder Roger Moens to take the gold medal in an Olympic best 1 min 46.3 sec. It was the launch of an international career in which Snell proved himself one of the greatest 'big occasion' competitors of all time. He was never once beaten in a race that really mattered and he won all his five major championship events: the 1960 Olympic 800 metres, the 1962 Commonwealth 880 yards and mile and the 1964 Olympic 800 metres and 1,500 metres.

Like Herb Elliott, Snell had a fitness fanatic coach providing his main motivation. Arthur Lydiard had been one of New Zealand's outstanding marathon runners in the immediate post-war years and he perfected training methods that enabled his athletes to build up enormous reserves of stamina. Even for a half miler and miler like

Snell, Lydiard believed in long-distance running as the surest way to reach peak condition. Before going to Rome to tackle the 800 metres, Snell was running up to 100 miles a week including gruelling uphill hauls over a 22-mile circuit in the Waitakere Ranges outside Auckland. Few athletes in the Rome Games had done so much thorough preparation work and this is why Snell and Lydiard were quietly confident that they could startle the favourites for the gold medal. As well as having good basic speed, he was a powerfully sculptured man who had immense strength that time and again worked to his advantage in tight finishes.

He revealed his potential as a miler when helping the New Zealand quartet set a world record in

3 54.1

*Snell (No. 466) used the same winning tactics in both the 800 metres final (left) and the 1,500 metres final (above) in the 1964 Tokyo Olympics. He was content just to sit behind the leaders and then used his strength and speed to pulverise his rivals over the last 200 metres.*

the 4 x 1 mile relay in Dublin on 17 July 1961. Yet he had never broken the four-minute barrier when he lined up for the start of a mile race on the 385-yard grass track at Wanganui on 27 January 1962. He clocked a breathtaking 3 min 54.4 sec, clipping Herb Elliott's world record by 0.1 sec. The world wanted to see a confrontation between Snell and Elliott but the Australian had bowed out of athletics and nothing could tempt him back into the competitive arena. Just seven days after his mile triumph, 'Pell-Mell' Snell was back in record-breaking mood. He produced a sensational solo run in Christchurch, leading from gun to tape to win the 880 yards in a world record 1 min 45.1 sec. On the way he knocked 1.4 sec off the world best for

800 metres. He then went on a tiring tour of the United States where he took on and beat the best milers America could produce. When the 1962 Commonwealth Games were staged in Perth it was rumoured that he had burnt himself out in the States but he made nonsense of those stories by winning the gold medals in both the 880 yards and mile finals.

The 1964 Tokyo Olympics were Snell's next major target and he poured himself into a training programme that was so punishing that the actual races would prove a blessed release from the self-inflicted torture. He knew that he had to be at a physical and psychological peak because he was aiming for the 'impossible' double of the 800 and

45

*A golden moment for Snell as he wins the Olympic 1,500 metres title at the 1964 Tokyo Games.*

1,500 metres gold medals. This had not been achieved in an Olympics since Britain's Albert Hill had won both events in the 1920 Games in Antwerp. But it was considered beyond anybody in the modern Games because it demanded six high-pressure races in just eight days. First of all, Snell defended the 800 metres title he had won in Rome as an unknown. Now he was the most famed and feared two-lap runner in the world and a marked man for all the challengers for his crown. Few of them saw anything but the back of his black vest. He won his heat in a comfortable 1 min 49.0 sec and his semi-final in an impressive 1 min 46.9 sec. It was expected that he would be hard pressed to win the final where Jamaican George Kerr and Kenyan

Wilson Kiprugut were highly fancied to give him a tough race. But Snell saw them off in style. He powered into the lead with 200 metres to go and went away to win in an Olympic record 1 min 45.1 sec, the fastest time in history apart from his world record run.

The determined New Zealander's job was only half completed and he was back in action the next day, easily qualifying for the semi-finals of the 1,500 metres in his first ever race at the distance. He took a 24 hours breather and then won his semi-final in a fast 3 min 38.8 sec. Would he have the strength and energy left to win the final and a third gold medal? This was the question everybody was asking on the final day of the track and field programme when Snell lined up in a high-calibre field that included his countryman John Davies, Czech ace Josef Odlozil and Britons John Whetton and Alan Simpson. In pre-race interviews it was clear that Snell was feeling the pressure. 'It's much, much worse than in Rome four years ago,' he said. 'I will not be prepared to go through this sort of thing again. Everybody expects so much and I'm sick to death of having the name of Herb Elliott thrust at me. What do I have to do to get rid of his image?' Snell came up with the answer himself. He won the 1,500 metres championship in the sort of majestic manner that meant he no longer had to live in Elliott's shadow but could be held up as at least his equal. He timed his finish to perfection, unleashing a final 200 metres in 25.4 sec to win in 3 min 38.1 sec with Odlozil just pipping his fellow New Zealander John Davies for second place seven metres behind. It was a proud day for New Zealanders and revived memories of Jack Lovelock's gold medal success in the 1936 Berlin Olympic 1,500 metres.

Snell had unkind critics who grumbled that he did only enough to win instead of going all out to break Elliott's world record. But he had the satisfaction of knowing he had achieved what he had set out to do in Tokyo, winning the golden double and almost toying with the world's finest middle-distance runners in the process. A month later in New Zealand and still running on the reserves he had built up in his torturous preparation for the Olympics, Snell set a new world record for the 1,000 metres and then the following week brought his own world mile record down to 3 min 54.1 sec. But all his hard work was taking its toll and it was no secret that he was losing his appetite for running. He had made many sacrifices and his work was suffering as was proved when he failed his exams as a quantity surveyor. He tried to revive his flagging interest by going on a tour of the United States and Europe but the spark had gone out of his stride and defeats by up-and-coming American teenager Jim Ryun convinced him the time had come to hang up his spikes.

Like Herb Elliott – the man in whose shadow he had to live – Snell went into retirement leaving the belief among athletics followers that he had not reached his absolute peak. So often in his major races he had not been pushed to the limit and had gone through the tape seemingly with yards in hand. But he achieved enough to be rated with the very greatest of the golden milers. In all, he ran eleven sub-four minute miles and was never beaten when it really mattered.

# FOR THE RECORD

*Snell prepares to receive the first of his three Olympic gold medals after the 1960 800 metres final in Rome.*

Peter Snell was born at Opunake, New Zealand, on 17 December 1938. He concentrated as a youngster on lawn tennis and did not switch seriously to athletics until he was 18. He proved he had character and courage to go with his natural ability when he overcame a stress fracture of a bone in his foot to qualify for New Zealand's team in the 1960 Rome Olympics.

These were his major victories:

| DATE | VENUE AND EVENT | TIME |
|---|---|---|
| 2. 9.60 | Rome, 800 metres | 1 min 46.3 sec (Olympic final) |
| 27. 1.62 | Wanganui, 1 mile | 3 min 54.4 sec (World record) |
| 3. 2.62 | Christchurch, 880 yards* | 1 min 45.1 sec (World record) |
| 27.11.62 | Perth, 880 yards | 1 min 47.6 sec (Commonwealth Games final) |
| 1.12.62 | Perth, 1 mile | 4 min 4.6 sec (Commonwealth Games final) |
| 16.10.64 | Tokyo, 800 metres | 1 min 45.1 sec (Olympic final) |
| 21.10.64 | Tokyo, 1,500 metres | 3 min 38.8 sec (Olympic final) |
| 12.11.64 | Auckland, 1,000 metres | 2 min 16.6 sec (World record) |
| 17.11.64 | Auckland, 1 mile | 3 min 54.1 sec (World record) |

*He also set a world record at 800 metres of 1 min 44.3 sec.

Snell's best times in non-specialist events were: 440 yards 47.9 sec; 3,000 metres steeplechase 9 min 38.8 sec and marathon 2 hours 41 min 11 sec.

He was a member of the New Zealand team that broke the world 4 x 1 mile relay record in Dublin on 17 July 1961, and was clocked at 1 min 44.9 sec when running an 880 yard relay leg in London shortly after the 1960 Rome Olympics.

*Michel Jazy . . . the track idol of France who set six world records in his birthday month of June.*

# MICHEL
# JAZY
## 3 53.6

JUNE WAS A MAGIC MONTH for Michel Jazy, the track idol of France who was at his most impressive when running against the clock rather than flesh-and-blood opposition. Jazy set seven world records during his illustrious long-running career and all but one of them came in his birthday month of June. He also had a share of an eighth world record when he was the main motivator for the French national 4 x 1,500 metres relay team that set a new world best time of 14 min 49.0 sec in 1965. The month, of course, was June.

The son of an immigrant miner from Poland and a French mother, Jazy was drawn to athletics by the inspiring performances of French-Algerian Alain Mimoun in the 1952 Olympics when he won silver medals in the 5,000 and 10,000 metres behind bouncing Czech Emil Zatopek. Jazy was then 16 and showed rich potential in his very first race when he won a 3,000 metres cross-country event. Coached by the knowledgeable René Frassinelli, he became French 1,500 metres champion in 1956 and later in the year joined his hero Mimoun in the team bound for the Melbourne Olympics. Mimoun won the marathon gold medal but Jazy's inexperience was exposed in the 1,500 metres when he finished seventh in his heat. Over the next two years his strength, stamina and tactical understanding grew while he was doing his compulsory military service. His mental as well as his physical approach to running was improved by sessions with highly-regarded coaches Woldemar Gerschler and Gosta Olander, who were both renowned as makers of champions.

When he left the forces, he was given an undemanding job on the esteemed French sports paper *L'Equipe* where most of his energies were spent on sharpening his speed and increasing his endurance. Proof that his specialised training was having the right effect came in the 1960 Rome Olympics. He took the silver medal in the 1,500 metres behind runaway winner Herb Elliott. Jazy returned home to Paris wiser and more determined for his experience in Rome. 'Herb Elliott has proved to me that I have still got a lot more work to do,' he said. 'I will now set my sights on the 1964 Olympics in Tokyo.'

Two years later Jazy set about rewriting the record books and proving that he had moved up into the Elliott class. He created a new world best for 2,000 metres in 5 min 1.6 sec on 14 June 1962, and on 27 June set a new record for the 3,000

*Jazy ... better attuned to running against the clock than man.*

metres with a time of 7 min 49.2 sec. The flying Frenchman then went to Belgrade and won the European 1,500 metres title in 3 min 40.9 sec. In June 1963, he added the world two-miles record (8

*Record-breaker Jazy clipped half a second off Peter Snell's world mile best with a time of 3 min 53.6 sec.*

min 29.6 sec) to his collection and ran a European best for 1,500 metres. He was widely tipped to win the gold medal in the 1964 Olympic 1,500 metres but he surprisingly elected instead to bid for the 5,000 metres title. It led to the most disappointing moment of his career. He ran the perfect race up to the bell and then committed the tactical error of taking the lead too early and with a spurt that was in no way conclusive. He did not have the strength to maintain his long run for the tape and he was overtaken first by crack German Harald Norpoth and then by under-rated American Bob Schul, who unleashed his positive challenge coming off the final bend. Schul went away from Norpoth to win by three metres, with his 30-year-old American team-mate Bill Dellinger driving past the shattered Jazy to snatch third place. It was Jazy who had started the mad scramble for home at the bell and the final lap was covered in an exceptionally fast 54.8 sec.

Defeat came like a knife thrust to Jazy who had set his heart on a gold medal victory in Tokyo. He talked during the depths of a post-race depression of retiring from competitive running but was so overwhelmed by messages of encouragement from his army of supporters in France that he decided to carry on. He vowed that he would step up his training and create more world records. He provided action to go with his words and in the following season set no fewer than ten European and three world records with a one-man running blitz that was quite astonishing considering his disillusionment after his comparative failure in the 1964 Olympics. His most incredible performance came in the mile on 9 June 1965. He clipped half a second off Peter Snell's world record with a time of 3 min 53.6 sec on a rutted track at Rennes that did not seem suitable for competitive athletics let alone such an outstanding record run. Jazy ran like a man inspired and timed his final sprint to perfection to prove that he was better attuned to running against the clock than man. 'Perhaps I should have gone for the 1,500 metres title in last year's Olympics,' Jazy admitted with a rueful smile after his record-shattering display.

Fourteen days later Jazy and Australian Ron

51

*The two great clockwork men of the track ... Jazy and Ron Clarke in a two-mile race that the Frenchman won in a new world record.*

Clarke, the two greatest 'clock-watchers' in athletics, were brought together for a fascinating confrontation over two miles at Melun. Both men were at their absolute peak. Clarke had been gathering world records in even more impressive fashion than Jazy. He had proved himself the fastest man in the world over three miles, 5,000 metres, six miles, 10,000 metres, 10 miles, 20,000 metres and had also crammed most miles into an hour. Jazy made a mockery of those critics who dismissed him as a mechanical robot runner with a stunning performance that left Clarke trailing. The Frenchman went through 3,000 metres in a world record 7 min 49.0 sec and completed the two miles in a world's best 8 min 22.6 sec. Later in the season, Jazy was matched with Kenyan sensation Kipchoge Keino and also saw him off in style.

In the 1966 European championships in Budapest, Jazy made a brave bid for a double in the 1,500 metres and 5,000 metres. West German Bodo Tummler outsprinted him in a thrilling finish to the 1,500 metres but Jazy struck gold in the 5,000 metres. He won a superbly judged race in 13 min 42.8 sec which was exactly six seconds faster than Bob Schul's victory time in the 1964 Olympic 5,000 metres final. His French fans were hoping that their idol would keep on running and show the world that he was not just a clockwork runner. They talked enthusiastically of how he could win a gold medal in the 1968 Mexico Olympics to wipe out the memory of his disappointment in Tokyo. But Jazy, at 30, knew that an Olympic title in Mexico was beyond him and he announced that he would bow out of international athletics at the end of 1966. With typical flair, he decided to go out with a bang and set out to recapture his world 2,000 metres record that had been lowered to 4 min 57.8 sec by West German Harald Norpoth on 10 September 1966. It was the first time the five-minute barrier had been broken. For once, Jazy did not wait for his favourite month of June in which to make his record attempt. He lined up in a specially staged race at St Maur des Fosses on 12 October 1966. It was out of season but he produced a per-

*Bob Schul ... the American who broke Jazy's heart in the 1964 Olympics.*

formance that ranked alongside his world mile record run.

Jazy clocked an incredible 4 min 56.2 sec, which meant he had maintained sub-four minute mile speed for nearly a mile and a quarter. It was a world record that stood the test of time for ten years before at last being beaten by New Zealander John Walker. It was a fitting finale to Jazy's career that had been all about breaking records.

# FOR THE RECORD

Michel Jazy was born in Oignies, France, on 13 June 1936. He started competitive running at the age of 16 in 1952 and these were the seven world records he set during his distinguished 14-year track career:

| DATE | VENUE AND EVENT | TIME |
|------|-----------------|------|
| 14.6.62 | Paris, 2,000 metres | 5 min 1.6 sec |
| 27.6.62 | Paris, 3,000 metres | 7 min 49.2 sec |
| 6.6.63 | Melun, 2 miles | 8 min 29.6 sec |
| 9.6.65 | Rennes, 1 mile | 3 min 53.6 sec |
| 23.6.65 | Melun, 3,000 metres | 7 min 49.0 sec* |
| 23.6.65 | Melun, 2 miles | 8 min 22.6 sec* |
| 12.10.66 | St Maur, 2,000 metres | 4 min 56.2 sec |

*Both records set in the same race

Jazy ran the third leg for the French national team that broke the world 4 x 1,500 metres relay record at St Maur on 25 June 1965. Their time was 14 min 49.0 sec.

His record in major championships was: 1960 Rome Olympic 1,500 metres, second in 3 min 38.4 sec; 1964 Tokyo Olympic 5,000 metres, fourth in 13 min 49.8 sec; 1962 European championships (Belgrade) 1,500 metres, first in 3 min 40.9 sec; 1966 European championships (Budapest) 1,500 metres, second in 3 min 42.2 sec, 5,000 metres, first in 13 min 42.8 sec.

Curiously, another great French idol – 1976 Olympic 110 metres hurdles gold medallist Guy Drut – was born in the very same street in the small French town of Oignies where Jazy had been born 14 years earlier.

*Jim Ryun . . . the greatest miler in
American track history.*

# JIM
# RYUN
## 3 51.1

THE WORLD SAT UP and took notice when Jim Ryun broke the four minute mile barrier on 5 June 1964. He was just seventeen-years-old and still at school. Over the next three years he developed into the greatest miler in American track history, wiped out Herb Elliott's prodigious 1,500 metres world record and brought the 3 min 50 sec mile within range. Nobody could have guessed such golden glory awaited Ryun when he made his miling debut in a high school race at his home town of Wichita, Kansas, on 7 September 1962. A gangling, 6 ft 1 in 15-year-old, he had no strength in his long legs and finished way down the field in fourteenth place in a time of 5 min 38 sec. Less than five years later he had lowered his best time to a dazzling world record 3 min 51.1 sec.

Many youngsters would have found an alternative outlet for their energies after that first disheartening mile run but the long-legged Ryun – nicknamed the 'Stork in Shorts' – was determined to make the school track team. 'There is a magic about the mile,' he said some years later. 'I found myself dreaming of the day that I could get under four minutes. It was a dream that drove me on in all my many long, lonely hours of training.' Even while still at school, he was runing up to 15 miles a day in training. He followed a programme mapped out for him by coach Bob Timmons, whose demand-

*Ryun crosses the finishing line in the 1968 Olympic 1,500 metres final but with 'only' a silver medal to show for his effort. Kip Keino had taken the gold three seconds earlier. Germany's Bodo Tummler took the bronze.*

ing methods brought a lot of criticism from other less adventurous coaches. His methods also brought startling results.

Ryun's progress under Timmons' tutelage was spectacular. Within six months, he had chopped his best time to 4 min 26.4 sec and on 8 June 1963, he recorded 4 min 07.8 sec. He was just five weeks past his sixteenth birthday. Timmons gave him a winter workload that involved running more than 100 miles a week, with stamina training mixed in with speed work. 'I knew that Jim was something extra special,' the coach said. 'On the rare days when he was finding it hard going I motivated him by reminding him of the goal he had set himself. The four minute mile. He accepted that there was no substitute for work, work and then more work. I knew it was physically possible for a high school runner to break four minutes provided he was properly conditioned. I also knew that in Jim Ryun I had found a richly talented performer who would prove my theory correct. He had the ability, he had the dream and he had the desire. I just showed him the way.'

Ryun's long, hard winter brought a summertime of great achievement. His dream of a four minute mile came true with a run of 3 min 59 sec and he qualified for the United States 1964 Olympic squad with a 3 min 39 sec 1,500 metres that was the equivalent of a 3 min 57 sec mile. The Tokyo Games were too soon for him and, handicapped by a streaming cold, he finished last in his semi-final. Peter Snell, the 1964 Olympic champion, looked in a completely different class to him. Yet before the

*A rare shot of Jim Ryun standing still!*

next year was halfway through he had left a below-par Snell floundering in a race in the States. Ryun won two sub-four minute miles in June 1965, and had now beaten the 'dream' barrier five times. And each time he had gone faster, coming down from 3 min 59 sec to 3 min 55.3 sec. He was just eighteen.

There was no stopping Ryun in 1966. Now a slim but powerful 6 ft 2 in and 160 lb, he revealed his basic speed when lowering the 880 yards world record to 1 min 44.9 sec at Terre Haute, Indiana, on 10 June 1966. He followed this with a magnificent mile run at Berkeley, California, on 17 July 1966, when he shattered Michel Jazy's world record with a time of 3 min 51.3 sec. It is interesting to compare Ryun's breakdown figures with those of some of his predecessors as world mile record holders:

| QUARTER | HAEG | BANNISTER | LANDY | ELLIOTT | RYUN |
|---|---|---|---|---|---|
| 1st 440 | 56.6 sec | 57.5 sec | 58.5 sec | 58.0 sec | 57.9 sec |
| 2nd 440 | 61.9 sec | 60.7 sec | 60.2 sec | 60.0 sec | 57.6 sec |
| 3rd 440 | 61.7 sec | 62.3 sec | 58.5 sec | 61.0 sec | 59.8 sec |
| 4th 440 | 61.7 sec | 58.9 sec | 60.6 sec | 55.5 sec | 56.0 sec |
| Record | 4:01.4 | 3:59.4 | 3:57.9 | 3:54.5 | 3:51.3 |

Ryun was the second world mile record holder to come out of Kansas. But while his predecessor Glenn Cunningham (see *Forerunners*) was known

*Kip Keino . . . runaway winner of the 1968 Olympic 1,500 metres final.*

*The Stork in Shorts who had winged feet.*

as the 'Iron Horse' of the track, Ryun was more of a smooth Wichita express, who could get up phenomenal speed when at full steam. He proved this at Bakersfield, California, on 23 June 1967, when he chopped his mile record to 3 min 51.1 sec. His last lap was run in a breath-taking 52.5 sec. Herb Elliott's world 1,500 metres record, set when he won the gold medal in the 1960 Olympics, was Ryun's next target. It was considered one of the safest records in the book but he made it look almost ordinary by cleaving two and a half seconds off it with a time of 3 min 33.1 sec. This record run came on 8 July 1967, when he was representing the United States against a British Commonwealth team. Left 15 metres adrift as the Wichita Wonder kicked for home was Kenyan Kip Keino.

Few could have envisaged Keino being able to

*How the mighty are fallen: Jim Ryun tumbles to the track in a heat of the 1,500 metres in the 1972 Olympics and lies in agony (above). American protests failed to get him reinstated.*

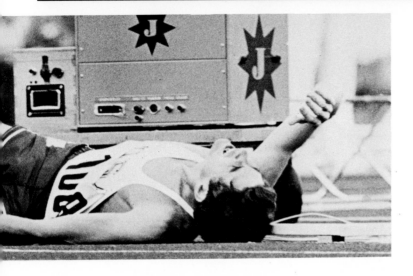

avenge this crushing defeat by Ryun in the 1968 Olympics even though they were being staged at altitude. But the young American was never again able to scale the peaks of 1966 and 1967. An attack of glandular fever robbed him of his snap and sparkle and he struggled to qualify for the US Olympic team. With his team-mate Ben Jipcho helping to take the strain, Kip Keino set out in the 1,500 metres final with the vowed intent to run the feared finishing kick out of Ryun. Jipcho took the field through a fast first lap in 56 seconds and then, with two laps to go, Keino moved to the front and quickly opened a commanding lead. Ryun had been content to cruise along with the back markers and suddenly found himself 25 metres adrift of the Kenyan, who lived at altitude and was having no problems coping with the thin air. It was not until after the bell that Ryun made his familiar finishing spurt but Keino had already got the gold in his grasp and he went through the tape 20 metres clear in 3 min 34.9 sec, a personal and Olympic best performance. Ryun produced a last lap of 55.7 sec to take the silver medal in 3 min 37.8 sec, 4.7 sec slower than his world record. He was heavily and unfairly criticised for his tactics but it was a creditable performance considering the high altitude and the fact that six months earlier it had looked certain that illness was going to knock him out of the Olympics.

He started to have psychological as well as physical problems in 1969. He failed to complete several races and when he walked off the track during the 1969 American mile championship most people thought he was finished with international athletics. But Ryun was once again a young man with a dream. Instead of a four-minute mile, his dream was now of an Olympic gold medal. He took an 18-month break from running and then returned in the winter of 1971 for a series of superb indoor performances, including equalling the world indoor mile record of 3 min 56.4 sec. His sights were set on the Munich Olympics.

But his dream turned into a nightmare in the 1972 Games. He had driven himself harder than ever before to get into the right shape to win the elusive 1,500 metres title for America for the first time since Mel Sheppard's victory back in 1908. He had the talent but not the luck. Ryun fell following a collision in his heat and was unable to catch the leaders in what should have been a simple qualification race. American officials protested on his behalf but the Olympic judges refused to give Ryun a second chance. Ryun gave up his dream and turned professional. He bowed out leaving us with memories of a master miler whose teenage track exploits are legendary.

## FOR THE RECORD

Jim Ryun was born in Wichita, Kansas, on 29 April 1947. His progress as a teenage miler was quite phenomenal as this time-and-age table shows:

| DATE | AGE | TIME |
|------|-----|------|
| 7.9.62 | 15 | 5 min 38.0 sec |
| 28.3.63 | 15 | 4 min 26.4 sec |
| 3.5.63 | 16 | 4 min 16.2 sec |
| 25.5.63 | 16 | 4 min 08.2 sec |
| 8.6.63 | 16 | 4 min 07.8 sec |
| 16.5.64 | 17 | 4 min 06.4 sec |
| 23.5.64 | 17 | 4 min 01.7 sec |
| 5.6.64 | 17 | 3 min 59.0 sec |
| 15.5.65 | 18 | 3 min 58.3 sec |
| 29.5.65 | 18 | 3 min 58.1 sec |
| 4.6.65 | 18 | 3 min 56.8 sec |
| 27.6.65 | 18 | 3 min 55.3 sec |
| 4.6.66 | 19 | 3 min 53.7 sec |
| 17.7.66 | 19 | 3 min 51.3 sec (World record) |
| 23.6.67 | 20 | 3 min 51.1 sec (World record) |

Ryun also set world records at 1,500 metres (3 min 33.1 sec) and 880 yards (1 min 44.9 sec). His best time over two miles was 8 min 25.2 sec and his fastest 5,000 metres run was clocked at 13 min 38.2 sec.

In February 1971, he equalled the then world indoor mile record with a time of 3 min 56.4 sec. His silver medal in the 1,500 metres in the 1968 Olympics in Mexico was won in 3 min 37.8 sec. He had a brief professional career with the International Track Association which went out of existence in 1976.

*Filbert Bayi . . . who electrified athletics with his catch-me-if-you-can tactics.*

**FILBERT**
**BAYI**
3 51.0

# BAYI

F EW ATHLETES HAVE MADE such a meteoric rise to
world fame as Filbert Bayi (pronounced *Bye-ee*). The 19-year-old Tanzanian failed to
survive his heats in the 1972 Olympic 1,500 metres
and steeplechase, yet within a matter of months
had eclipsed Kenyan track king Kip Keino as
Africa's new middle-distance sensation. Bayi announced his arrival as a world-class athlete when
he left the veteran Keino trailing on his way to the
African 1,500 metres championship in 3 min 37.2
sec. Later in 1973 he made a triumphant tour of
Europe in which he confirmed his world status. He
adopted dramatic catch-me-if-you-can tactics, setting an electric pace from gun to tape and rarely
finding anybody who could stay with him.

His courageous front running brought him a
Commonwealth 1,500 metres record of 3 min 34.6
sec when he went through 400 metres in 53.6 sec,
800 metres in 1 min 51.6 sec and 1,200 metres in 2
min 52.2 sec. Cynics described his methods as

*Portrait of a panther ... Bayi in reflective mood before a training workout.*

suicidal and predicted he would be setting himself
up as purely a pacemaker for anyone with a 'kick'
finish. There was a hint that perhaps Bayi *was*
being naive with his tactics in a mile just a few days
later when he again set off like a hare. This time
Kenyan Ben Jipcho hung on his heels and sprinted
past him on the final lap to win in 3 min 52.0 sec.
Bayi finished in 3 min 52.6 sec but was still convinced that his way was the most effective way. It
certainly provided great viewing for the spectators
but would it work in a major championship against
top-quality opposition? The answer came in the
Commonwealth Games 1,500 metres final in
Christchurch, New Zealand, on 2 February 1974.

John Walker, the latest track idol of New
Zealand, was among Bayi's rivals and had proved
in an impressive string of victories that he had the
sort of devastating finish that could torpedo the
brave Tanzanian. But Bayi was tuned to perfection
for the race after months of dawn runs at a high-
lands training camp near Mount Kilimanjaro.
Predictably, he sped into the lead right from the
gun in Christchurch and went through 400 metres
in 54.4 sec and 800 metres in 1 min 51.8 sec. He
opened a long lead on Walker but everybody was
expecting him to start to fade. There was a startling contrast in the styles and approach of Bayi and
Walker. The Tanzanian air force officer almost
glided around the track, with a lightweight,
feathery step. His slender features expressed no

*It was Kip Keino (576) who led the black explosion in middle distance running
but he had to be content with second place in this 1972 Olympic 1,500 metres
final. Finland's Pekka Vasala (226) is just unleashing his winning kick for
home.*

*The race that made Bayi a world star . . . victory in the 1974 Commonwealth Games 1,500 metres final ahead of Kiwis John Walker and Rod Dixon. Bayi's time was a world record 3 min 32.3 sec.*

emotion or strain and his 5 ft 9 in, 135 lb frame was perfectly balanced as he went into the final lap with a commanding lead. Walker, a grimacing, grunting and totally committed competitor, was using all the strength and speed he could muster from his powerful 6 ft 1 in, 165 lb physique as he pounded the track in pursuit of the flying African. With an almost super-human effort, Walker began to chop down the lead and it looked as if he might just catch Bayi. But the Tanzanian kept his head and his pace and broke the tape in a world record 3 min 32.2 sec. Walker, at the end of a glorious race, was just two metres behind and also finished inside the old world record with a time of 3 min 32.5 sec. They had a re-match later in the year in Helsinki. This time Walker refused to let Bayi get away from him and the African had no answer when the New Zealander spurted away on the last lap to win in 3 min 33.4 sec. Now the world waited for the show-down between the two marvellously matched rivals in the 1976 Montreal Olympics.

They whetted appetites further with some scintillating performances in 1975. Bayi clipped a tenth of a second off Jim Ryun's world record with a 3 min 51.0 sec run in Jamaica on 17 May. His lap times were 56.9 sec, 59.7 sec, 58.7 sec and 55.7 sec.

*Bayi drives for the tape and victory in the 1975 Emsley Carr mile at Crystal Palace. Young, bearded Steve Ovett was overtaken by Scotland's Ian Stewart and Poland's Bronislaw Malinowski (11).*

*As usual, Bayi is the pace setter in this 1980 Golden Mile but it was Steve Ovett who came through to win.*

The record lasted less than three months, with Walker taking it down through the 3 min 50 sec barrier (see *John Walker*). Several promoters tried to get Walker and Bayi together on the track again but the combination of malaria (Bayi's) and Achilles tendon problems (Walker's) kept them apart. Everything was set for the decisive duel in the Montreal Games but providence and politics continued to treat them unkindly. Tanzania joined the African boycott of the Olympics because of the IOC's refusal to bar New Zealand for allowing a Rugby Union team to tour apartheid-practising South Africa and the Bayi-Walker clash was off.

Bayi shrugged off his disappointment. 'I was looking forward to running against Walker,' he said, 'but that is not the most important thing to me. We have to fight against apartheid.' Walker was, typically, more outspoken. 'We're sportsmen,' he fumed. 'It's bloody ridiculous to turn us into politicians.'

To prove he had beaten his illness and an injury that cut short a European tour, Bayi unleashed a 1,500 metres in 3 min 34.8 sec in 1976 – nearly five seconds faster than Walker's winning time in the Olympic 1,500 metres final. There was consolation for Bayi. Missing the Olympics meant he could bring forward his marriage which he had originally postponed until after the Montreal Games because he had been leading a monastic life in the Tanzanian training camp in the foothills of Mount Kilimanjaro.

The exploits of Sebastian Coe and Steve Ovett over 1,500 metres in the build-up to the 1980 Moscow Olympics convinced Bayi that he would be more likely to strike gold by aiming for the 3,000 metres steeplechase title. He had taken little interest in the gruelling event after his unsuccessful attempt to get past the heats in the 1972 Olympics in Munich. He made up his mind to treat it seriously after winning a steeplechase in Stockholm in July 1980, in a tremendously fast 8 min 18.0 sec. Bayi ran the steeplechase the same way he ran all his races, from the front and as fast as his legs would carry him. His technique left a lot to be desired but his sheer speed made up for the vital seconds he lost at the hurdles. In his heat in the Moscow Games he was inside a world record schedule for most of the race but slowed down over the last two laps to win in 8 min 21.4 sec. At the last minute, he scratched from the 1,500 metres. He was pinning all his medal hopes on the steeple-

*Bayi . . . making a splash in the steeplechase.*

*Bronislaw Malinowski . . . outsmarted Bayi in the 1980 Olympic steeplechase final. Sadly, he died in a car crash the following year.*

chase where his rivals included the formidable Pole Bronislaw Malinowski and Ethiopian Eshetu Tura who crossed the line with Bayi in the semifinal in 8 min 16.2 sec.

Bayi set off at the gun in the final as if his life depended on victory. He continued to lose time at each of the hurdles, clearing them with a scissors technique as if competing in the high jump. But he was impressive with the strength of his leap over the water-jump and his speed on the flat was so quick that with just two laps to go he was 35 metres in the clear and looking a certainty for gold. But the canny old fox Malinowski was now in pursuit, overtaking the tiring Tura and gradually closing

the gap between him and Bayi whose usual smooth gait was beginning to look distinctly heavy and uneven. Malinowski drew level with Bayi just before the water-jump and then sprinted unchallenged into the lead, taking the Olympic title in 8 min 09.7 sec with Bayi a disappointed second in 8 min 12.5 sec.

The son of a proud Scottish mother, Malinowski kissed his gold medal after the presentation ceremony and said: 'I trusted myself all the time. I remembered how Bayi had come back in his second race against John Walker and knew he would come back to me. He was setting too fast a pace and I refused to panic even when the lead stretched to more than twenty-five metres.' Sadly, Malinowski died the following year in a car crash. The memory lives on of his genius as a tactician. As the sporting Bayi commented after he collected his silver medal: 'Bronislaw set out to run the race the way *he* wanted to and refused to let me disrupt his plan. I had set my heart on winning the gold medal but at least I have the consolation of knowing I was beaten by a great champion.'

Like Bannister, Landy, Jazy and Ryun before him, Bayi seemed likely to leave the world stage as one of the finest middle-distance runners *never* to win an Olympic gold medal. But the style, spirit and speed of his running meant he would never be forgotten by the men he ran against and the spectators he thrilled with his follow-the-leader tactics.

# FOR THE RECORD

Filbert Bayi was born at Karatu on 22 June 1953. He ran his first major 1,500 metres race at the age of 17 in 1970 and was clocked at a very modest 4 min 07.2 sec. The following year he had got his personal best time down to 3 min 52.0 sec. He qualified for the 1972 Tanzanian Olympic team in both the 1,500 metres and the 3,000 metres steeplechase. He revealed his promise with times of 3 min 45.4 sec for the metric mile and 8 min 41.4 sec in the steeplechase but failed to survive his heats. These have been his most outstanding performances:

| YEAR | EVENT | TIME |
|---|---|---|
| 1973 | 1,500 metres | 3 min 37.2 sec (SA title) |
| 1973 | 1,500 metres | 3 min 34.6 sec (C'wealth record) |
| 1974 | 1,500 metres* | 3 min 32.2 sec (World record) |
| 1975 | 1 mile | 3 min 51.0 sec (World record) |
| 1976 | 1 mile (indoors) | 3 min 56.1 sec (US indoor title) |
| 1976 | 1,500 metres | 3 min 34.8 sec |
| 1977 | 5,000 metres | 13 min 20.7 sec |
| 1978 | 1,500 metres | 3 min 35.6 sec (2nd Commonwealth Games) |
| 1980 | 3,000 metres steeplechase | 8 min 12.5 sec (2nd Olympic Games) |

*Won Commonwealth Games gold medal

Bayi tried his usual front-running tactics in a bid to burn off the opposition when defending his 1,500 metres title in the 1978 Commonwealth Games in Edmonton. He went through 400 metres in 57.7 sec, 800 metres in 1 min 55.2 sec and 1,200 metres in 2 min 53.9 sec but was unable to shake off Scot John Robson and England's Dave Moorcroft who won a thrilling three-man battle down the finishing straight to win in 3 min 35.5 sec with Bayi a stride behind in second place and just one-hundredth of a second ahead of Robson. Thanks once again to Bayi's bold running, it was the fastest and most exciting 1,500 metres race of the year. Proving his versatility, Bayi also had an 800 metres personal best time of 1 min 45.3 sec.

*John Walker . . . the first man to break the 3 min 50 sec barrier.*

# JOHN
# WALKER
3 49.4

JOHN WALKER IS THE THIRD MEMBER of the great New Zealand 'Triumphant Triumvirate' of world record-breaking milers who also won golden glory in the Olympic 1,500 metres. He took over the torch lit by Jack Lovelock in the 1930s and which was handed on by Peter Snell in the 1960s. His lasting fame is assured because he was the first man to break the 3 min 50 sec barrier.

Walker has brought a touch of glamour to the track. He has long, blond hair that flows like a sail in the wind when he is at full speed and he does not give the impression of treating running as a life-or-death matter. The man in black is a throwback to the run-for-fun champions like Chris Chataway, Derek Ibbotson and Ronnie Delany who could smile in defeat as well as victory. He gives his racing and training the total dedication and commitment they need but he also finds time for an enjoyable social life and his notorious roistering has often made his rivals wonder how he has managed to stay in the top-flight of milers for more than six years. The answer is simply that he has great natural speed, stamina and strength allied to a tremendous resolve. Walker himself has put it like this: 'I attribute seventy per cent of my ability

*. . . great natural speed, strength and stamina . . .*

to inheritance. My father was a champion cyclist, excellent runner and a good tennis player. The rest is down to a grinding slog in training for 21 hours a week.' He has also proved he has character to go with his talent, battling through injury problems that would have forced men with less determination into retirement.

It was in defeat that the world was alerted to Walker's class and fighting qualities. The way he chased Filbert Bayi to a world record in the 1974 Commonwealth Games 1,500 metres final revealed that here was a man well capable of carrying on the tradition of great New Zealand milers. Walker took over as the king in 1975 during a barnstorming tour of Europe. He just missed Bayi's 1,500 metres world record in July when he clocked 3 min 32.4 sec and then two weeks later, on 12 August, he pushed back the boundaries of the mile to under 3 min 50 sec with a sensational run in Gothenburg. Paced through the first quarter-mile in 55.8 sec and the half-mile in 1 min 55.1 sec, Walker was left to go it alone for the second half of the race and in a long, lonely drive he reached the bell in 2 min 53.0 sec and covered the last lap in 56.4 sec for a history-making final time of 3 min 49.4 sec. It was exactly

*. . . long blond hair that flows like a sail in the wind when he is at full speed . . .*

*Walker (694) is poised to challenge for the lead in the semi-final of the 1976 Montreal Olympic 1,500 metres. Steve Ovett (375) was pushed back to sixth place and failed to qualify for the final.*

ten seconds faster than Roger Bannister's first four minute mile 21 years earlier.

Coached by the demanding Arch Jelley, Walker made no secret of the fact that he was aiming for a gold medal in the 1976 Olympic 1,500 metres. He piled in the miles in both training and competition in a search for peak conditioning. He finished fourth in the IAAF cross-country championship in the winter of 1975 and completed a 21-mile run at 2 hr 19 min marathon tempo. One of the main motivating factors for him was the prospect of a deciding third meeting in the Olympics with his great rival Filbert Bayi. The score between them was one race each and Walker and his coach were thinking in terms of a remarkable 3 min 30 sec victory target. This did not seem too far fetched when Walker produced a 2,000 metres run on 30 June 1976, that was every bit as impressive as his mile performance in Sweden ten months earlier. He

chopped an incredible 4.8 seconds off Michel Jazy's world record in Oslo, producing lap times of 60.1 sec, 58.5 sec, 57.7 sec, 57.9 sec and 57.2 sec. He ran the final mile in a fraction outside 3 min 53 sec! What made his 4 min 51.4 sec run even more incredible was that conditions in Oslo were windy and hardly conducive to world record breaking.

Just five days later in Stockholm, he won the 1,500 metres in 3 min 34.2 sec which was the fastest metric mile of the year. He was really wound up for his Olympic duel with Bayi in Montreal and it was a terrible anti-climax for him when Tanzania joined the African boycott of the Games. Walker was bidding for the 800-1,500 double, last performed in the Olympics by his countryman Peter Snell in Tokyo in 1964. Weakened by illness, he gave a sluggish show in the 800 metres and was eliminated in the heats on the opening day. He was back to full fitness in time for the 1,500 metres and

*John Walker strikes gold in the 1,500 metres final in the 1976 Montreal Olympics. He is chased to the tape (bottom right) by Ivo Van Damme, Paul Heinz Wellmann, Frank Clement and Eamonn Coghlan.*

won his heat in 3 min 36.9 sec and his semi-final in 3 min 39.7 sec. Run out of it in sixth place in his semi-final was a young British runner called Steve Ovett. With no Filbert Bayi to set his customary lightning pace, the final developed into a slow tactical battle. Walker was content to sit and conserve his energy as the field proceeded in a shuffling, nervous fashion that produced the slowest Olympic winning time for 20 years. The 3 min 30 sec 1,500 metres was to remain the 'impossible' dream, and the spectators and competitors were left to wonder on what might have been had Bayi been around to stir things up.

Walker played the waiting game until, with 250 metres to go, he produced his famed and feared finishing burst that – because of the leisurely pace – looked even more spectacular than usual. Plenty of his rivals also had a lot of gas left and gave him a hard chase but he had the strength and the speed to get to the line first in 3 min 39.2 sec. Belgian Ivo

*The new Olympic champion checks the scoreboard just to make sure he's not dreaming (top right) but the presentation of the gold medal provides all the proof he needs that he has carried on the great New Zealand traditions in the metric mile*

Van Damme (who was tragically to die in a car crash the following year) took second place to add to the silver medal he had won in the 800 metres. It was far from the most devastating performance of Walker's career but he had the immense satisfaction of reaching his target of the gold medal. 'This is what matters most to me,' he said later, holding up his medal. 'I've been working hard for it for four years and I am delighted and proud to have won it for New Zealand. I was very conscious of the traditions I had to maintain and I am pleased and relieved that I was able to do what my countrymen Jack Lovelock and Peter Snell had done before me.' Asked if Bayi's absence had knocked the gloss off his victory, Walker shrugged and said: 'The only way my day would have been spoilt is if I had failed to take the gold medal. I beat the other runners in the Final. I could do no more than that. I'm not interested in talking about hypothetical cases. I'm an athlete not a politician and my only thought before the race was on beating the other competitors. I was not thinking about which runners were not taking part. Looking back, I think I can say the best thing that happened to me was going out of the 800 on the first day. It proved a blessing in disguise because I was able to give all my concentration and effort to the 1,500. That was the one I really wanted to win.'

Ironically and sadly, Walker himself was prevented by the poison of politics from taking part in the Moscow Olympics where he had been hoping to become the first 1,500 metre champion to retain his title. In protest against Russia's invasion of

*...and has brought a touch of glamour to the track...*

Afghanistan, Walker chose not to run in Moscow. He had started to show a return to his old form after hospital treatment for a recurring leg injury but – I hope without being accused of British bias – I doubt if he would have been able to master the dual challenge of Sebastian Coe and Steve Ovett in Moscow.

But that, as Walker would be quick to point out, is hypothetical. In Montreal, he produced the winning form where and when it mattered and nobody can take away from him the fact that he was the man who showed the way through the 3 min 50 sec mile barrier. He can stand proudly alongside Jack Lovelock and Peter Snell as the third and fastest of New Zealand's truly *golden milers.*

# FOR THE RECORD

John Walker was born at Papukura, New Zealand, on 12 January 1952. His father was a top-class all-round sportsman and he grew up in a sports-dominated environment. Inspired by Peter Snell's 1964 Olympic triumphs in the 800 and 1,500 metres, he started to take a close interest in running and showed he had rich potential when running a 3 min 52.4 sec metric mile in 1970. By 1975, he had got that time down to 3 min 32.5 sec. His personal best over 800 metres was 1 min 44.9 sec. These have been among his outstanding performances:

| YEAR | EVENT | TIME |
|------|-------|------|
| 1974 | 1,500 metres | 3 min 32.5 sec (2nd Commonwealth Games |
| 1974 | 1 mile | 3 min 54.9 sec |
| 1975 | 1,500 metres | 3 min 32.4 sec |
| 1975 | 1 mile | 3 min 49.4 sec (World record) |
| 1976 | 2,000 metres | 4 min 51.4 sec (World record) |
| 1976 | 1,500 metres | 3 min 39.2 sec (Olympic gold medal) |
| 1977 | 1,500 metres | 3 min 32.7 sec (Fastest that year) |
| 1977 | 1 mile | 3 min 52.0 sec (Fastest that year) |

Walker was then plagued by injuries and also seemed jaded by so much competitive running. He dramatically dropped out of a World Cup 1,500 metres on the final bend as Steve Ovett went away to win in style. But he happily rehabilitated himself in September 1977, with a 3,000 metres victory at London's Crystal Palace in 7 min 41.9 sec. After hospital treatment on his troublesome leg injuries, he bravely returned to international competition but was overshadowed by the emergence of Ovett and Sebastian Coe as the new miling masters. But Walker was still a formidable force as he proved with a series of sub-four minute miles and a world indoor best for 1,500 metres of 3 min 37.4 sec at Long Beach, California in 1979.

*Sebastian Coe welcomes his Olympic 1,500 metres gold medal triumph with open arms, while East Germany's Jurgen Straub beats Steve Ovett for the silver medal.*

**SEBASTIAN** **STEVE**

# COE OVETT

3 47.33

THERE CAN BE NO separating Steve Ovett and Sebastian Coe, the majestic milers whose almost parallel track careers have had a thunder and lightning effect on world athletics. Coe has been the lightning to Ovett's thunder as they have swopped the world mile record like men locked in the fastest game of musical chairs on earth. Here's how they have brought the record down to within striding distance of the 3 min 45 sec barrier:

17.7.79: Sebastian Coe 3 min 48.95 sec (Oslo)
 1.7.80: Steve Ovett    3 min 48.80 sec (Oslo)
19.8.81: Sebastian Coe 3 min 48.53 sec (Zurich)
26.8.81: Steve Ovett    3 min 48.40 sec (Koblenz)
28.8.81: Sebastian Coe 3 min 47.33 sec (Brussels)

Getting these two great British rivals together on the same starting line has proved beyond the ability of even the most enterprising promoters. As I write, their racing paths have never crossed over the mile and entrepreneurs lick their lips at the prospect of a meeting that would fill any stadium in the world and attract a massive TV audience. They have raced against each other three times (not including a 1972 English schools cross-country race; Ovett, 11 months older, came second; Coe finished tenth) and always in major championships when the title rather than the time was uppermost in the minds of all the competitors. Their rivalry first became a magnet for wide public interest when they clashed in the 1978 European 800 metres final in Prague.

Coe was then the European indoor champion and the UK record holder over 800 metres at 1 min 45.0 sec. Ovett was the UK record holder over both the mile (3 min 54.7 sec) and the 1,500 metres (3 min 34.5 sec). They were so conscious of each other's ability in the European final that they handed the race to powerful East German Olaf Beyer. The two Britons were so busy watching each other that they failed to see Beyer coming up on the outside off the final bend and were unable to respond as he sprinted past them 25 metres from the tape. Ovett won his personal duel with Coe, beating him for second place by two metres in 1 min 44.1 sec. He then gained revenge over Beyer in the 1,500 metres final and later in the same month set a UK record for the mile in Oslo (3 min 52.8 sec), ran a world outdoor best two miles to conquer the great Henry Rono in London (8 min 13.5 sec) and won the Golden Mile in Tokyo when clocking his tenth sub-four minute mile in four years (3 min 55.5 sec). Coe created a new UK 800 metres record of 1 min 44.0 sec but 1978 was indisputably Ovett's year.

Yet for all his success, Ovett remained an almost unknown, enigmatic figure off the track. He was embroiled in a feud with many of the leading national newspaper athletics correspondents, refusing to give the customary post-race interviews because he had been so angered and hurt by critical articles back in 1975. At least he was consistent with his vow of silence, declining to attend formal dinners, social functions and televised award presentations. Coe, meanwhile, was proving himself the most approachable, likeable and image-conscious British athlete ever to make an impact on the world stage and the media made the most of his inviting personality. This all led unfairly to Ovett being blackened with the 'villain's' reputation in what was becoming a media-made 'good guy v. bad guy' situation. They were getting the sort of attention and projection usually associated with world championship boxing opponents. In fighting terms, it would have to be a catchweight contest. Coe is an 8 st 8 lb bantamweight, 5 ft 9 in tall and with a smooth stride that gives him greater lever-

*Coe . . . approachable, likeable and image conscious.*

age than many bigger men because of a bounding style that has been perfected in many hours of 'leg speed' work at Loughborough College under the supervision of George Gandy, a specialist in bio-mechanics. Ovett is a 6 ft 1 in, 11 st light-middle-weight who is one of the most naturally gifted athletes ever to step foot on a running track. He has been a winner all his life, from early schoolboy days and few runners in the world can match his versatility. His successes range from victories over 400 metres to a win in a 13-mile half-marathon.

While Coe is outgoing and friendly, Ovett is an introverted character but seemingly with a show-man buried somewhere deep inside him. He has been known to go months without giving an inter-view and then suddenly draw attention to himself with outspoken comments that cause ripples of un-rest among officialdom or other athletes. Both men are extremely intelligent and articulate, with Coe always prepared to give an insight into his tactical thinking while Ovett is more reticent to open up but is worth listening to when he does break his self-imposed silence. Not only do they have con-trasting personalities and physiques but also approach their training with a different attitude. Coe, diligently coached by his father, Peter, has a programme geared to improving his muscular form and speed and he rarely covers more than 65 miles a week. Ovett, coached by the experienced Harry Wilson, sometimes runs more than 150 miles a week in his search for untapped stamina to go with his basic speed.

It is interesting to see how Coe's arrival as a world-class runner – a couple of years behind his rival – seemed to change Ovett's approach to athletics. He had always described himself as a 'racer', more interested in beating men than the clock. But the record book became more and more of an attraction for him as Coe started to produce performances that in turn pushed the Brighton art student towards new, unexplored territories. Not since the days of the Bannister/Landy rivalry had two milers given the media so much contrasting material to set before a hero-hungry public and it was the courteous Coe, of the pleasant smile and affable manner, who clearly came across as the Fleet Street favourite. If it had been a Victorian melodrama, you could imagine Coe coming on to the track to cheers while for Ovett there would be jeers and the traditional hisses.

Ovett was quietly amused by the contrasting picture being painted by the Press and did little off the track to tip the balance of publicity his way. He infuriated promoters all round the world by often preferring to turn out for a club meeting in Brighton rather than run at international jam-borees, competing for Brighton and Hove Athletic Club and, more recently, the Phoenix team he helped to form. Quietly and without fuss, he did his own public-relations job by working hard for charitable organisations (particularly for the dis-abled) and by never refusing an autograph even though it often sometimes meant as much as an hour spent under siege from signature hunters. The 'bad guy' was not all bad, although occasion-ally his brazen cockiness on the track – waving to the crowd as he arrogantly swept past outpaced opponents – went beyond showmanship into the area of poor taste.

The publicity spotlight switched almost exclu-sively on to 'good guy' Coe during an astonishing span of 41 days in the summer of 1979 when he set new world records for 800 metres (1 min 42.4 sec), 1,500 metres (3 min 32.1 sec) and the mile (3 min 48.95 sec). Ovett's stunning reply came in July the following year when he lowered the mile record (3 min 48.8 sec) and equalled Coe's 1,500 metres

*Steve Ovett . . . a naturally gifted athlete.*

79

*Coe and Ovett . . . locked in the fastest game of musical chairs on earth.*

*Ovet (375) finished fifth in the 1976 Olympic 800 metres final and was pushed back to sixth place in this 1,500 metres semi-final.*

world best. Coe refused to be left out in the cold and chipped in with a world record 1,000 metres (2 min 13.4 sec). It all brought interest in their 1980 Moscow Olympic rivalry to fever pitch. The popular forecasts were that Coe would win the gold medal in the 800 metres and Ovett the 1,500 metres. British appetites were satisfied to the point that they did win an Olympic title each but not the way most experts expected. Coe, in his own words, ran like 'a chump and a novice' in the final of the 800 metres when Ovett proved himself much better at looking after himself in a physically tough race where elbows appeared to be used as weapons. The 'Brighton Express' powered to victory in 1 min 45.4 sec, with Coe delivering his attack far too late and having to make do with second place.

It was not the *fastest* of Olympic finals but certainly one of the *fiercest*. At times it had looked more like a loose maul in a rugby match than an athletics race. Henry Cooper, former British heavyweight boxing hero, was in Moscow with the BBC *Sport-on-2* radio team and was moved to comment: 'Blimey, I've seen less physical contact in fights in the ring. I thought these blokes were supposed to be gentlemen. Ovett knew how to use his elbows. Coe didn't. That was the big difference.'

Within minutes of Ovett winning the race, the East German and French officials were threatening protests over his tough tactics. But all Ovett had been guilty of was protecting himself in a battle in which sportsmanship took second place to a win-at-all-costs mood that seemed to eat into all the competitors, with the exception of Coe who made no impact on the race until his desperate spurt·off the final bend. The protest threats were never made official and Ovett deservedly collected a gold medal for which he had worked furiously hard. Declining to attend the post-race Press conference, Ovett told ITV commentator Adrian Metcalfe in an exclusive interview: 'I was possibly guilty of doing more pushing than most but I honestly think everyone ran a fair race. You've got to bear in mind that all the athletes are wearing long spikes and if anybody gets close to you it's an instinctive thing to fend them off because they are dangerous. It might look bad to people watching but it's just safety precautions.'

David Miller, *Daily Express* correspondent, one of the most authoritative of all Fleet Street sportswriters, has collaborated on a revealing and informative book with Sebastian Coe called *Running Free* (Sidgwick & Jackson). In it, Coe says of the

800 metres: 'Only after I had seen the video recording of the race did I realise how physical Steve had been. I felt it had contributed to the tattiness of the race. It lowered the standing of athletics.

'I was very surprised that the East Germans and French didn't make more of it. I would hate to think that as a result of that final we might breed a race of middle-distance runners who breast-stroke their way out of a scrum. The 800 metres is unique because nowadays it is almost a sprint the whole way, just not in the lanes for the last 670 metres. It's eight guys fighting for a position in a sprint spread over two-and-a-half lanes. Of course you have to react tactically, and I didn't. But if you accept the development of physical contact, then tactics mean nothing, and the roughest man is going to win. You cannot equate racing ability with handing people off, as some of the press did. It is tactically allowable to protect the space you have earned by your pace or your positioning, but *not* to

*Another first for Coe as he wins the 1979 European Cup 800 metres final for Britain.*

*Ovett tracks Henry Rono and prepares to unleash his famous winning kick.*

83

gain space that is occupied by somebody else which you would prefer. That is not tactical intelligence, it's the negation of it.'

The articulate and highly intelligent Coe wisely kept these thoughts to himself until the Moscow Games were over, otherwise he would have risked a charge of sour grapes. He still had a job to do in Moscow and he buried himself in his preparations.

The silver medal in the 800 metres represented abject failure for Coe. It brought cutting comment from Peter Coe, his main motivator and coach: 'Sebastian ran like a blockhead. I just couldn't believe it. He got everything wrong. It wouldn't have been so bad had it been an exceptionally fast world record pace but to lose like this is inexplicable. He is quite rightly disgusted with himself.' Coe still had a chance to redeem himself in the 1,500 metres but few would have backed him against Ovett. He was looking relaxed and full of running and was even winning the hearts and affection of the millions watching on television as he ended each race by sending an 'I Love You' signal to his girlfriend (now his wife) Rachel, who was at home in Brighton. Suddenly there was a reversal of roles and this time there had been no image manufacturing by the media. 'Bad Guy' Ovett had taken over the saintly mantle, while Coe went into a deep depression over his appalling – by his perfectionist standards – performance in the 800 final.

It looked as if his hopes and dreams of an Olympic gold medal had gone because the supremely confident Ovett had put together a stunning sequence of 45 mile and 1,500 metre races without a single defeat. But we all underestimated the tremendous character and determination of the student from Sheffield. East German Jurgen Straub boldly led the field for three minutes of the final. Then it became Coe's glorious race. He attacked like a demon off the middle of the last bend. This time, there would be no tactical mistakes. He smoothly moved up a gear as he hit the final straight and went away from Straub. Ovett tried to give chase but as it became obvious that there was no catching the flying figure of Coe he relaxed and allowed Straub to hold him off in the race for the silver medal. There was only going to be one winner and as Coe crossed the finishing line his arms were outstretched as if miming a crucifixion and his face was creased with a mixture of ecstasy and emotional exhaustion.

He had poured every ounce of his being into the race of a lifetime and was mentally and physically shattered as he dropped to his knees on to the track. Straub and 'Good Guy' Ovett heartily congratulated him but he was now operating in a daze and hardly seemed to notice. He almost floated around on his lap of honour which was briefly interrupted for a victory hug from his tearful father. Sebastian

*The eyes of the world were on Ovett and Coe in Moscow where they won a gold medal each and confounded the experts.*

3 47.33

*The 1980 Olympic 800 metres final and Ovett is on his way to victory and the gold medal. Coe has started his challenge but too late . . .*

*Ovett first, Coe second . . . 'I ran like a chump and a novice,' said Coe.'*

Coe was like a man who had come back from the dead. 'He went through absolute purgatory between the two finals,' Peter Coe said later. 'His rise from the deepest of deep depressions to a will to win was just unbelievable.'Coe himself said: 'I came here to Moscow interested only in winning a gold medal. I blew it in the 800 by running like a chump. It made me all the more determined to win the 1,500. Now I can live with myself and I am free to run as I please.'

Coe's winning time of 3 min 38.4 sec was six seconds outside his world record for the metric mile. But the clock did not matter, only the winning counted and he had done that in regal style. While the time was fairly modest by world-class standards, track statisticians realised they had witnessed something special when they made a study of the 'splits'. Coe had run the last 800 metres in an astonishing 1 min 48.5 sec, the fastest two laps ever run in a three-and-a-half or four lap race. His phenomenal sprinting ability was shown over the last 200 metres which he covered in 24.7 seconds, with the final 100 metres completed in just 12.1 seconds.

'I have to admit I was too self confident before the 800 metres and ran like a man having a doze,' Coe said. 'But the 1,500 metres made up for it all. It went exactly as I wished. Thanks to the pace set by Straub I was able to run relaxed and free. Steve Ovett, Steve Cram and I had all wished each other luck on the starting line. I knew it was a race I HAD to win and gave it everything. About 20 or so metres from the tape I felt absolutely shattered and knew I had nothing left if anybody came back at me but I had managed to kill them all off with two kicks for home, the first 180 metres out when I went past Straub and then again as I came off the final bend. All the anxiety I felt was mirrored in my face as I crossed the line at the finish. It was a mixture of pain and pure, marvellous relief.'

Straub, the East German whose brave front-running had made a real race of it, celebrated as if he had collected the gold medal when he held off Steve Ovett for second place. Straub was clocked at 3 min 38.8 sec, with Ovett just a fifth of a second slower in the bronze medal position.

It was a crazy reversal of form, because before the Moscow Games just about every track-and-field 'expert' was tipping Coe for the 800 metres and Ovett for the 1,500. Ovett shrugged off the disappointment of his defeat in his speciality race and said: 'I am equally happy about my gold and my

*Ovett's finger says it all: 'I'm number one'. Top left: Coe fights to hide his disappointment as he congratulates his great rival during the 800 metres awards ceremony.*

bronze because for both I did my best. I don't think anybody quite appreciates how lonely it is out there on the starting line before an Olympic final.

'For the first time in the 1,500 metres, I collapsed under pressure. I think Seb did the same in the 800 metres final. But he got it right in the 1,500. I realized at the beginning of the last straight that I was not going to catch him. I had given all I could.'

Little could anybody have guessed that this was all a prelude to a procession of even greater performances by both Coe and Ovett. They continually raced each other but on different tracks, driving each other to new peaks of achievement with times that were mind-blowing for track statisticians. Ovett brought the curtain down on a memorable 1980 by lowering Coe's world 1,500 metres record to 3 min 31.6 sec at Koblenz where West German doctor Thomas Wessinghage selflessly played the part of the sacrificial hare. Coe replied in the summer of 1981 with another hat-trick of world records. He chopped the 800 metres best down to an incredible 1 min 41.73 sec, pushed himself through a pain barrier to record 2 min 12.18 sec for 1,000 metres and then reduced Ovett's year-old mile

*The 1,500 metres final and revenge for Coe. He was always well positioned and made none of the tactical errors that destroyed his victory chances in the 800 metres.*

record to 3 min 48.53 sec. He was disappointed with this performance. His target had been to knock seconds off the old time but he had to be content with just a fraction and, on the way, had been well outside Ovett's 1,500 record. 'I can do much better than this,' Coe said in self-admonishment that personified his never-ending quest for perfection. There were two outstanding performances behind Coe. Kenyan Mike Boit, at 33, became only the sixth man in history to break the 3 min 50 sec barrier with a time of 3 min 49.74 sec. A stride behind in third place and setting a world's best for a 20-year-old of 3 min 49.95 sec came Jarrow's Steve Cram, surely a Golden Miler of tomorrow.

Just seven days later in Koblenz, the remarkable Ovett regained the mile record. Superbly paced by his friend and travelling companion Bob Benn and then American James Robinson, he covered the last lap in 57.78 sec to trim 0.13 sec off the time by Coe which was so new it had yet to be entered in any record books. There were suggestions afterwards that Ovett's latest record-busting feat might not be ratified because the race had not been officially mentioned in the meeting programme. But to all but the fastidious, the new world record *did* belong to Ovett at 3 min 48.53 sec. Before the 'is-it-or-isn't-it-a-record?' dispute could take root, the calculating Coe had rendered all argument a waste of breath. Running in the *Citizen Golden Mile* in Brussels barely 48 hours later, he brought the world record down to a staggering 3 min 47.33 sec. It was the third time he had set a world best for the mile, a triple triumph achieved before him only by Swedes Gundar Haegg and Arne Andersson. Tom Byers, who had helped Coe to his second world mile record, again did the major pacemaking in the early stages and took the field through a fast 54.92 sec first lap. Byers continued to lead at the half-mile mark in 1 min 52.6 sec and it was obvious that the record was within Coe's range. He quickly recovered after stumbling against the inside kerb and raced to the front as Byers slowed to a trot just before the bell. With the gallant Mike Boit chasing at his heels but never threatening to take the lead, Coe produced his famous acceleration and sped smoothly away to a win that knocked a phenomenal 1.07 seconds off Ovett's brand-new record. Boit finished second in 3 min 49.45 sec, which made him the fourth fastest miler of all time. American ace Steve Scott was third in 3 min 51.48 sec.

'Tom Byers deserves a lot of the credit for this

*Steve Cram (No. 8)...a Golden Miler of the future?*

record,' Coe said after his latest devastating performance. 'His magnificent early pace made it all possible.' He insisted that Ovett's new 48-hour-old record had not played a part in his motivation. 'I'm just sorry Steve wasn't competing here in this race,' he told reporters. 'The race would have been even faster with him in the field.'

Both Coe and Ovett were rewarded for their incredible running with an MBE each in the 1982 New Year Honours List, recognition that had been delayed following their refusal to listen to Prime Minister Margaret Thatcher's call for a boycott of the Moscow Olympics in protest at Russia's invasion of Afghanistan. The glory Coe and Ovett have brought to British sport in general, and athletics in particular, with their series of world records proved just impossible not to acknowledge.

They were in demand world wide and respected *Daily Mail* writers Ian Wooldridge and Neil Wilson revealed that negotiations were well advanced for them to meet in a three-race series worth minimally £1,250,000 in sponsorship and television rights, with much of the cash earmarked to be ploughed back into athletics – a prerequisite that Coe and Ovett would insist on because both of them are keen to put as much back into their sport as possible. To add further spice to their confrontation, it was reported that the Americans were pushing for black South African exile Sydney Maree to be included in the race series that was scheduled to be decided over 800 metres, one mile and 3,000 metres. Maree emerged in 1981 as the one man who could possibly challenge Coe and Ovett's standing as the world's top master milers. His application for American citizenship meant he was suddenly clear of the barriers of apartheid and able to show his paces against the best opposition outside South Africa – a country where the colour of his skin dictated where, when and against whom he could compete.

Maree revealed he was a miler with untapped potential when he handed Ovett a rare defeat in Rieti, Italy, on 9 September 1981. He celebrated his twenty-fifth birthday by outsprinting Ovett to win an invitation mile race in 3 min 48.83 sec, making him the third fastest miler of all time. Only Coe and Ovett have run faster and nobody has clocked a better time without breaking the world record. Ovett finished one-and-a-half seconds behind in 3 min 50.23 sec and commented: 'I am just too tired. I've had too many competitions in too few days and with too much travelling. I'm not in my best condition and need a rest.' Just four days earlier, Ovett

had beaten Maree with ease in the World Cup 1,500 metres on the same track.

If any further evidence of Maree's mile mastery was needed it came on the streets of New York just 17 days later. He beat a top-class field in a straight mile road race along Fifth Avenue to clock the second fastest mile in history: 3 min 47.52 sec.

Maree's emergence as a threat to their domination added new urgency to the preparations of Coe and Ovett for their record assaults in the summer of 1982. Ovett was handicapped by a nasty thigh muscle injury suffered when he slipped and fell into a church railing while on a training run near his Hove home. But he was confident he would be fit to defend his European 1,500 metres championship and to resume his rivalry with Coe.

There is no telling to what limits Coe and Ovett could push each other. With their speed, stamina and competitive spirit, the 3 min 45 sec mile and the 3 min 30 sec 1,500 metres are no longer fantasy. Both will go all out to produce the *unbeatable* mile time. Until the next Golden Miler comes along.

## FOR THE RECORD

STEVE OVETT was born in Brighton on 9 October 1955. He was an art student before switching full time to athletics. Coached by Harry Wilson, he stands 6 ft 1 in tall and weighs 11 st.

At 13 he was the fastest 400 metres runner of his age in Britain. He was a 17-year-old sixth former at Varndean Grammar School when he became the 1973 European junior 800 metre champion. In the 1976 Olympics he was fifth in the final of the 800 metres and reached the 1,500 metres semi-final. His outstanding performances:

| YEAR | EVENT/VENUE | TIME |
|---|---|---|
| 1977 | 1500 metres (Dusseldorf) (World Cup, UK record) | 3:34.5 |
| 1978 | 800 metres (Prague) (2nd European Champ., UK record) | 1:44.1 |
| 1978 | 1500 metres (Prague) (1st European Champ.) | 3:35.6 |
| 1978 | 1 mile (Oslo) (UK record) | 3:52.8 |
| 1978 | 2 miles (London) (World's outdoor best) | 8:13.5 |
| 1978 | 1 mile (Tokyo) (Golden Mile) | 3:55.5 |
| 1979 | 1 mile (London) | 3:49.6 |
| 1980 | 1 mile (Oslo) (World record) | 3:48.8 |
| 1980 | 1,500 Metres (Oslo) (Equalled World record) | 3:32.1 |
| 1980 | 800 metres (Moscow) (Olympic Games, 1st) | 1:45.4 |
| 1980 | 1500 metres (Moscow) (Olympic Games, 3rd) | 3:39.0 |
| 1980 | 1500 metres (Koblenz) (World record) | 3:31.6 |
| 1981 | 1 mile (Koblenz) (World record) | 3:48.53 |

SEBASTIAN COE was born in London on 29 September 1956. He is an economics graduate from Loughborough University. His home is in Sheffield where he is coached by his father, Peter. He is 5 ft 9 in and weighs 8½ st.

At 14 he won the Yorkshire schools cross country championship and two years later the Yorkshire schools 3,000 metres title, the English schools 3,000 metres title and the AAA youth 1500 metres championship. His first major senior victory was in the 1977 European indoor 800 metres final which he won in 1 min 46.54 sec. His record:

| YEAR | EVENT/VENUE | TIME |
|---|---|---|
| 1978 | 800 metres (London) (UK record) | 1:44.0 |
| 1978 | 800 metres (Prague) (European Champ., 3rd) | 1:44.8 |
| 1979 | 800 metres (Oslo) (World record) | 1:42.4 |
| 1979 | 1 mile (Oslo) (Golden Mile, World record) | 3:48.95 |
| 1979 | 1500 metres (Zurich) (World record) | 3:32.1 |
| 1980 | 1000 metres (Oslo) (World record) | 2:13.4 |
| 1980 | 800 metres (Moscow) (Olympic Games, 2nd) | 1:45.9 |
| 1980 | 1500 metres (Moscow) (Olympic Games, 1st) | 3:38.4 |
| 1981 | 800 metres (Cosford) (Indoor World record) | 1:46.0 |
| 1981 | 800 metres (World record) | 1:41.73 |
| 1981 | 1000 metres (World record) | 2:12.18 |
| 1981 | 1 mile (Zurich) (World record) | 3:48.53 |
| 1981 | 1 mile (Brussels) (Golden Mile, World record) | 3:47.33 |

# WORLD RECORDS

| TIME | RECORD HOLDER | DATE | VENUE |
|------|---------------|------|-------|
| 4:14.4 | **John Paul Jones** USA | 31.5.13 | Cambridge, Mass. |
| 4:12.6 | **Norman Taber** USA | 16.7.15 | Cambridge, Mass. |
| 4:10.4 | **Paavo Nurmi** Finland | 23.8.23 | Stockholm |
| 4:09.2 | **Jules Ladoumegue** France | 4.10.31 | Paris |
| 4:07.6 | **Jack Lovelock** New Zealand | 15.7.33 | Princeton, USA |
| 4:06.8 | **Glenn Cunningham** USA | 16.6.34 | Princeton, USA |
| 4:06.4 | **Sydney Wooderson** GB | 28.8.37 | Motspur Park, Surrey |
| 4:06.2 | **Gundar Haegg** Sweden | 1.7.42 | Gothenburg |
| 4:06.2 | **Arne Andersson** Sweden | 10.7.42 | Stockholm |
| 4:04.6 | **Gundar Haegg** Sweden | 4.9.42 | Stockholm |
| 4:02.6 | **Arne Andersson** Sweden | 1.7.43 | Gothenburg |
| 4:01.6 | **Arne Andersson** Sweden | 18.7.44 | Malmo |
| 4:01.4 | **Gundar Haegg** Sweden | 17.7.45 | Malmo |
| 3:59.4 | **Roger Bannister** GB | 6.5.54 | Iffley Road, Oxford |
| 3:57.9 | **John Landy** Australia | 21.6.54 | Turku, Fin. |
| 3:57.2 | **Derek Ibbotson** GB | 19.7.57 | White City, London |
| 3:54.5 | **Herb Elliott** Australia | 6.8.58 | Dublin |
| 3:54.4 | **Peter Snell** New Zealand | 27.1.62 | Wanganui, NZ |
| 3:54.1 | **Peter Snell** New Zealand | 17.11.64 | Auckland, NZ |
| 3:53.6 | **Michel Jazy** France | 9.6.65 | Rennes |
| 3:51.3 | **Jim Ryun** USA | 17.7.66 | Berkeley, Cal. |
| 3:51.1 | **Jim Ryun** USA | 23.6.67 | Bakersfield, Cal. |
| 3:51.0 | **Filbert Bayi** Tanzania | 17.5.75 | Kingston, Jam. |
| 3:49.4 | **John Walker** New Zealand | 12.8.75 | Gothenburg |
| 3:49.0 | **Sebastian Coe** GB | 17.7.79 | Oslo |
| 3:48.8 | **Steve Ovett** GB | 1.7.80 | Oslo |
| 3:48.53 | **Sebastian Coe** GB | 19.8.81 | Zurich |
| 3:48.40 | **Steve Ovett** GB | 26.8.81 | Koblenz |
| 3:47.33 | **Sebastian Coe** GB | 28.8.81 | Brussels |

# WORLD RECORDS

*(1,500 metres, which is just under 120 yards short of a mile. The usual conversion time for top-flight performances over a mile is 17.5 sec)*

| TIME | RECORD HOLDER | DATE | VENUE |
| --- | --- | --- | --- |
| 3:55.8 | **Abel Kiviat** USA | 8.6.12 | Cambridge, Mass |
| 3:54.7 | **John Zander** Sweden | 5.8.17 | Stockholm |
| 3:52.6 | **Paavo Nurmi** Finland | 19.6.24 | Helsinki |
| 3:51.0 | **Otto Peltzer** Germany | 11.9.26 | Berlin |
| 3:49.1 | **Jules Ladoumegue** France | 5.10.30 | Paris |
| 3:49.2 | **Luigi Beccali** Italy | 9.9.33 | Turin |
| 3:49.0 | **Luigi Beccali** Italy | 17.9.33 | Milan |
| 3:48.8 | **Bill Bonthron** USA | 30.6.34 | Milwaukee |
| 3:47.8 | **Jack Lovelock** New Zealand | 6.8.36 | Berlin |
| 3:47.6 | **Gundar Haegg** Sweden | 10.8.41 | Stockholm |
| 3:45.8 | **Gundar Haegg** Sweden | 17.7.42 | Stockholm |
| 3.45.0 | **Arne Andersson** Sweden | 17.8.43 | Gothenburg |
| 3:43.0 | **Gundar Haegg** Sweden | 7.7.44 | Gothenburg |
| 3:43.0 | **Lennart Strand** Sweden | 15.7.47 | Malmo |
| 3:43.0 | **Werner Lueg** Germany | 29.6.52 | Berlin |
| 3:42.8 | **Wes Santee** USA | 4.6.54 | Compton, USA |
| 3:41.8 | **John Landy** Australia | 21.6.54 | Turku, Fin. |
| 3:40.8 | **Sandor Iharos** Hungary | 28.7.55 | Helsinki |
| 3:40.8 | **Laszlo Tabori** Hungary | 6.9.55 | Oslo* |
| 3:40.8 | **Gunnar Nielsen** Denmark | 6.9.55 | Oslo* |
| 3:40.6 | **Istvan Rozsavolgyi** Hungary | 3.8.56 | Tata, Hungary |
| 3:40.2 | **Olavi Salsola** Finland | 11.7.57 | Turku, Fin.* |
| 3:40.2 | **Olavi Salonen** Finland | 11.7.57 | Turku, Fin.* |
| 3:38.1 | **Stanislav Jungwirth** Czech. | 12.7.57 | Stara Boleslav |
| 3:36.0 | **Herb Elliott** Australia | 28.8.58 | Gothenburg |
| 3:35.6 | **Herb Elliott** Australia | 6.9.60 | Rome |
| 3:33.2 | **Jim Ryun** USA | 8.7.67 | Los Angeles |
| 3:32.2 | **Filbert Bayi** Tanzania | 2.2.74 | Christchurch, NZ |
| 3:32.1 | **Sebastian Coe** GB | 15.8.79 | Oslo |
| 3:31.6 | **Steve Ovett** GB | 27.8.80 | Koblenz |

*Tabori and Nielsen set their records in the same race, as did Salsola and Salonen in 1957.

Mary Decker

Acknowledgements

The author wishes to thank Sir Roger
Bannister for his contribution to this
book and for his warm words of
encouragement. Thanks also to the
following authors whose informative
books and articles made research work
both easier and richly rewarding:
Sebastian Coe and David Miller,
*Running Free* (Sidgwick & Jackson,
1981); Sir Roger Bannister, *First Four
Minutes* (Putnam, 1955); Mel Watman
for various articles in his splendid
publication *Athletics Weekly*; Cliff
Temple for various articles in the
*Sunday Times*; the editors of *Sports
Illustrated*, *Track & Field News* and the
invaluable *L'Equipe*; also the editors of
the all-embracing Marshall Cavendish
encyclopedia of sport, *The Game*
(published in 112 parts, 1971/72).
Thanks, too, to Terry O'Connor, Rugby
and Athletics correspondent of the
*Daily Mail*, who interrupted my boring
verbal outflow of mile-race statistics in
1955 and told me bluntly: 'Don't *talk*
about it. *Write* it.' I've been a sports
writer ever since . . .

**B.B.C. Huyton Picture Library:** 15
(top left) 16, 20 (left).
**B.B.C. Stills Photo Library:** 78.
**Central Press:** 7, 18/19, 20 (right), 22,
23, 23, 25 (right), 26/27, 33, 51, 52, 64.
**Colour Sport:** Front jacket, 1, 54/55,
58/59, 60/61, 62 (left), 64/65, 70 (left),
71, 73 (insect bottom), 75, 82, 86/87, 89
(both), 91, 92.
**Focus on Sport New York:** Back
jacket flap, 96.
**E.D. Lacey:** 21, 25 (left), 30/31, 34,
36/37, 40 (right), 44, 44/45, 46, 48/49, 56
(right), 57 (right), 63.
**Sports Agence Magazine Paris:** Back
jacket, Front jacket flap, 2/3, 4/5, 6, 8/9,
10/11, 11, 12/13, 12 (inset), 14, 15 (top
right, bottom), 17, 32, 38, 39, 40 (left),
41, 42/43, 47, 50, 53, 56 (left), 57 (left),
62 (right), 66, 67, 68/69, 70 (right), 72/
73, 73 (inset top), 74 (both), 76/77, 79,
80/81, 83 (both), 84/85, 88, 90 (both)

How long before we see the first *woman* four
minute miler?

The present outdoor world record is held by
Russian Lyudmila Vesselkova who clocked 4 min
20.89 sec in the summer of 1981.

But most experts agree that if Russia's great
1,500 metre Olympic champion Tatyana Kazan-
kina wanted to make a concentrated attack on the
mile record she could bring it down to near 4 min 10
sec.

Her astonishing 1,500 metres world record of 3
min 52.5 sec is faster than the legendary Paavo
Nurmi ran the distance, and when she retained her
Olympic title in Moscow in 1980 she covered the
last 800 metres inside two minutes.

The best of the women milers outside Europe is
America's Mary Decker, who has been making impressive strides in recent seasons and will be
among the favourites for the 1,500 metres gold
medal at the 1984 Los Angeles Olympics.

She became the world's fastest woman miler in
February 1982, when she clocked a world indoor
best of 4 min 20.5 sec in San Diego.

Britain's Diane Leather was the first woman to
break the five-minute barrier with a time of 4 min
59.6 sec on 29 May 1954 – just 23 days after Roger
Bannister had broken four minutes for the first
time.